Children's First
ENCYCLOPEDIA

Written by
Claudia Martin

ARCTURUS

ARCTURUS

This edition published in 2023 by Arcturus Publishing Limited
26/27 Bickels Yard, 151–153 Bermondsey Street,
London SE1 3HA

Author and Editor: Claudia Martin
Designers: Amy McSimpson and Lorraine Inglis
Consultants: Jules Howard, Dougal Dixon, Chris Jarvis, and Dr. Helen Giles
Editors: Lucy Doncaster, Becca Clunes, and Lydia Halliday
Design Manager: Jessica Holliland
Editorial Manager: Joe Harris

ISBN: 978-1-3988-3111-7
CH011500NT
Supplier 29, Date 0923, PI 00004549

Printed in China

CONTENTS

INTRODUCTION

Let's get ready to set out on a voyage of discovery across time and space.

First, we'll explore the world in which we live—its weather, oceans, mountains, and deserts, as well as the natural disasters that can sometimes shake things up. We'll learn how hurricanes form, what the different habitats are called, and why most places on Earth experience different seasons.

Next, we'll blast off into space to take a look at the planets, moons, and other objects that exist both in our galaxy and beyond. We'll uncover the secrets of how it all began and the life cycle of stars. We'll marvel at rockets, telescopes, and all the amazing technology that makes space exploration possible.

We'll then come back down to Earth to examine the incredible world of animals. From the tiniest termite to the biggest elephant and everything in between, prepare to be dazzled by the mammals, fish, insects, amphibians, and other creatures that share our planet.

Finally, we'll time-travel to when dinosaurs roamed the Earth. We'll learn about the huge range of different types of dinosaurs, where they lived, how they behaved, and what they looked like.

So, what are you waiting for? Let's get going!

OUR WORLD

Our planet, called Earth, is just one of trillions of planets in the Universe. At the moment, we do not know of any other planet that is home to living things.

Earth is wrapped in a blanket of life-giving air.

Rocky Planet

Earth's rocky surface is shaped into high mountains, deep caves, and wide deserts. Sometimes, the rock shakes in terrifying earthquakes. Sometimes, melted rock explodes from volcanoes.

A climber tests his strength against our planet's beautiful, dangerous surface.

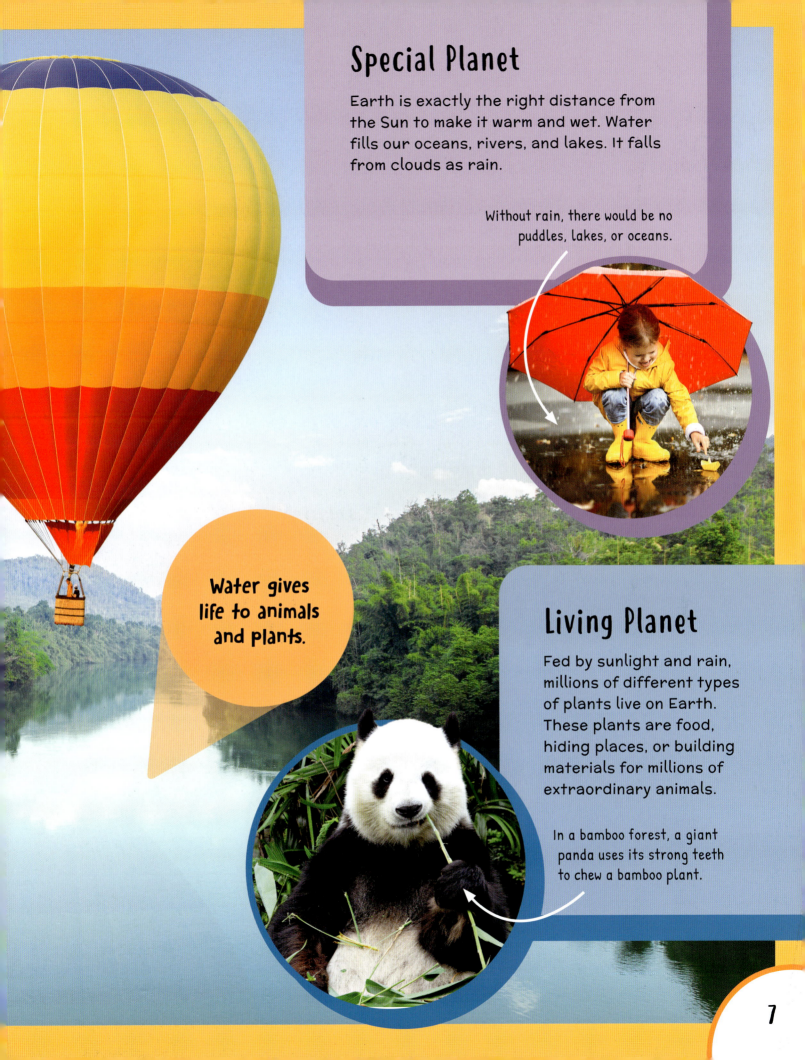

Special Planet

Earth is exactly the right distance from the Sun to make it warm and wet. Water fills our oceans, rivers, and lakes. It falls from clouds as rain.

Without rain, there would be no puddles, lakes, or oceans.

Water gives life to animals and plants.

Living Planet

Fed by sunlight and rain, millions of different types of plants live on Earth. These plants are food, hiding places, or building materials for millions of extraordinary animals.

In a bamboo forest, a giant panda uses its strong teeth to chew a bamboo plant.

OUR PLANET

Earth is one of eight planets spinning around a huge, hot star, called the Sun. Like all stars, the Sun is so hot that it glows, giving off light. At any time, one half of Earth is facing the Sun. This half of Earth has light, or daytime. The other half of Earth is in darkness, or nighttime.

As Earth turns, the Sun appears above the horizon at sunrise.

Turning

While Earth is moving around the Sun, it is also turning on its own axis (an imaginary line that runs through the North and South Poles). It takes 24 hours for Earth to make one complete turn.

Night follows day as Earth turns on its axis.

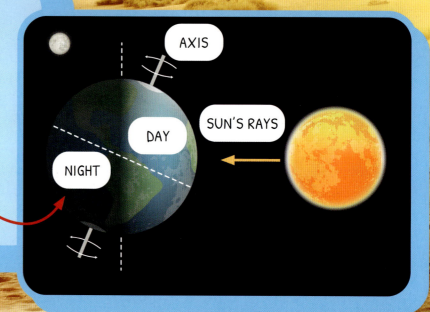

AXIS

DAY

SUN'S RAYS

NIGHT

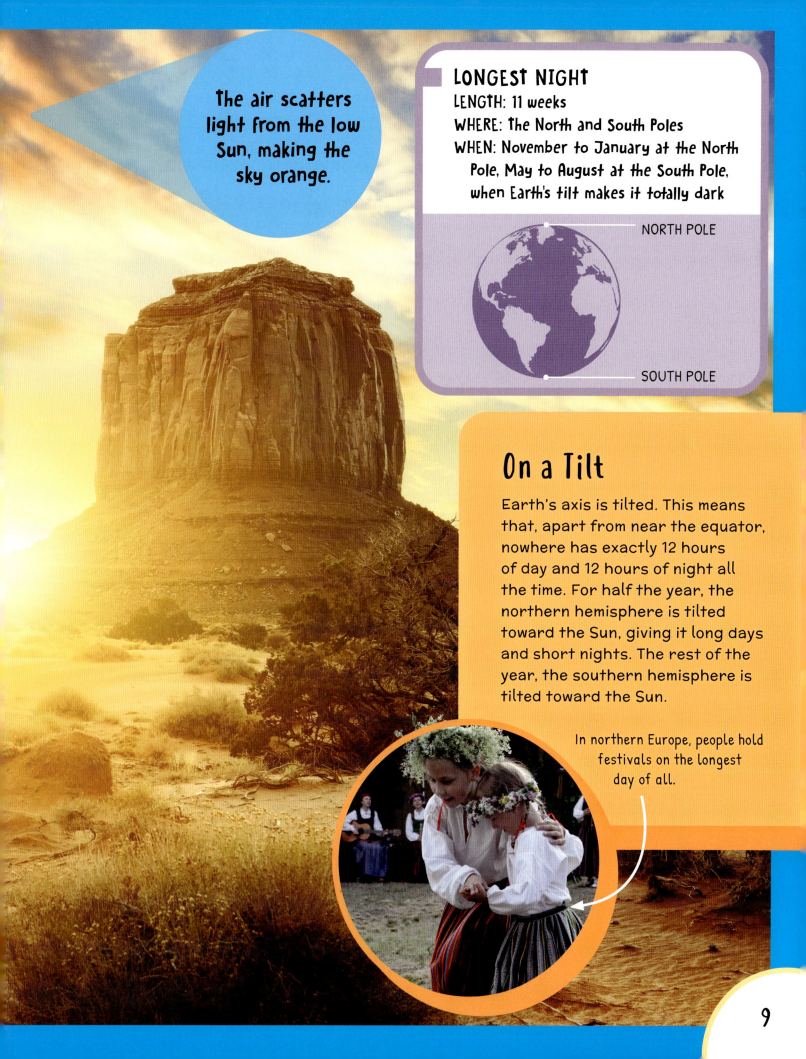

The air scatters light from the low Sun, making the sky orange.

NORTH POLE

SOUTH POLE

On a Tilt

Earth's axis is tilted. This means that, apart from near the equator, nowhere has exactly 12 hours of day and 12 hours of night all the time. For half the year, the northern hemisphere is tilted toward the Sun, giving it long days and short nights. The rest of the year, the southern hemisphere is tilted toward the Sun.

In northern Europe, people hold festivals on the longest day of all.

EARTH'S LAYERS

At the middle of the Earth is a ball of super-hot metal, called the core. Around the core is a layer of hot rock, called the mantle. Earth's outer layer, called the crust, is cool rock.

Metal Core

Earth's core is made mostly of the metals iron and nickel. In the outer core, the metal is so hot it is liquid. In the inner core, the metal is solid because it is squeezed too tight to melt.

When metal gets really hot, it melts—turning from a solid into a liquid.

THICKEST CRUST
THICKNESS: 70 km (43 miles)
WHERE: Under the Himalayan Mountains, Earth's tallest mountain range

— HIMALAYAS

The inner core is Earth's hottest layer, around 6,000 °C (10,800 °F).

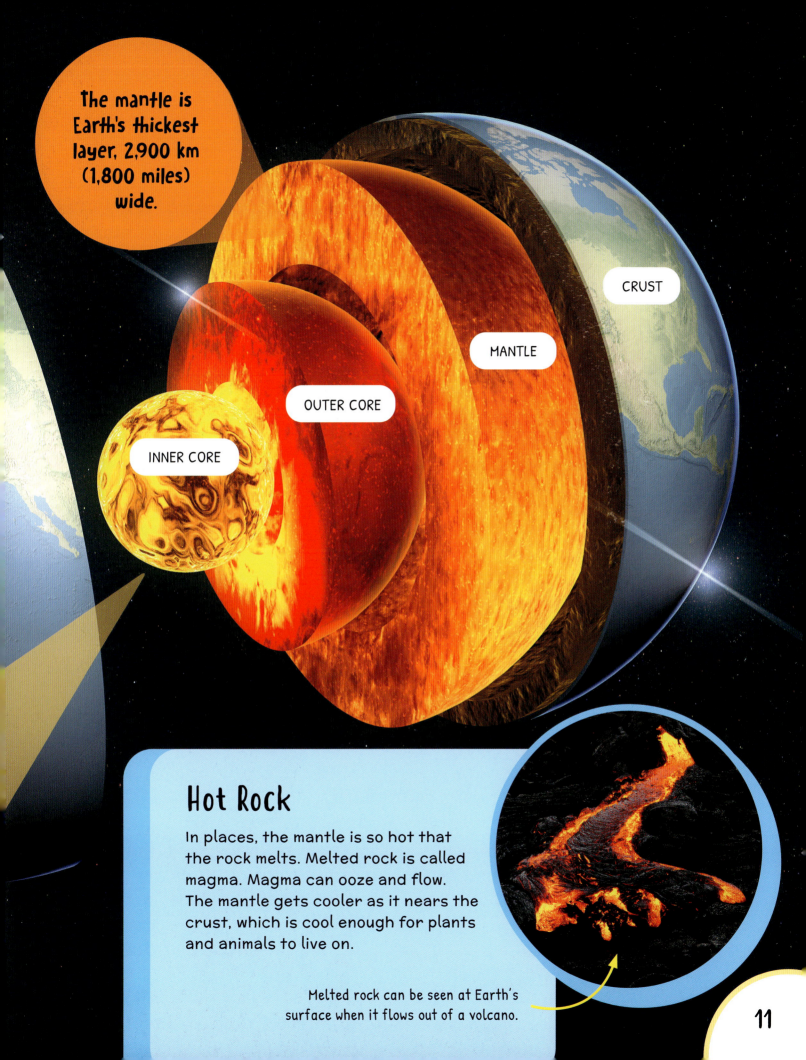

The mantle is Earth's thickest layer, 2,900 km (1,800 miles) wide.

CRUST

MANTLE

OUTER CORE

INNER CORE

Hot Rock

In places, the mantle is so hot that the rock melts. Melted rock is called magma. Magma can ooze and flow. The mantle gets cooler as it nears the crust, which is cool enough for plants and animals to live on.

Melted rock can be seen at Earth's surface when it flows out of a volcano.

11

ROCKS

Rock lies beneath the oceans, grass, and city streets. There are three types of rocks: igneous, sedimentary, and metamorphic. Each type was made in a different way.

The Giant's Causeway, in Northern Ireland, is made of the igneous rock basalt.

Three Rock Types

Igneous rock is made when magma cools and hardens. Sedimentary rock is made when bits of rock, dead animals, or plants are pressed together until they harden. Metamorphic rock is made when any rock is changed by heat and pressure underground.

These cliffs are made of limestone, a sedimentary rock. It can be formed when shells pile up on the seafloor, then are pressed together over a long period of time.

Useful Rocks

Granite and other strong rocks are cut from the ground, then used to construct buildings. Slate is a waterproof rock that is often used for roofing. Marble and other smooth rocks can be carved into sculptures.

A sculptor is working with marble. This metamorphic rock is made when limestone is heated and pressed.

OLDEST ROCK
AGE: 3.5 to 4 billion years old
ROCK: Gneiss, a metamorphic rock
WHERE: Slave Craton, northwest Canada

SLAVE CRATON

Melted rock ran out of a volcano, then cracked into regular shapes as it cooled.

OCEANS

More than two-thirds of Earth's surface is covered by water. Most of that water is saltwater, which fills giant basins in Earth's crust. This saltwater forms a huge world ocean.

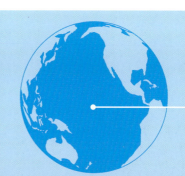

LARGEST OCEAN
AREA: 165,250,000 sq km
(63,800,000 sq miles)
NAME: the Pacific Ocean

PACIFIC OCEAN

Five Oceans

People usually divide the world ocean into five parts: the Pacific, Atlantic, Indian, Southern, and Arctic Oceans. Smaller areas of saltwater that are partly or totally surrounded by land are called seas.

This village is in the shallow water around Borneo, in the Pacific Ocean. The ocean gives the villagers fish to eat.

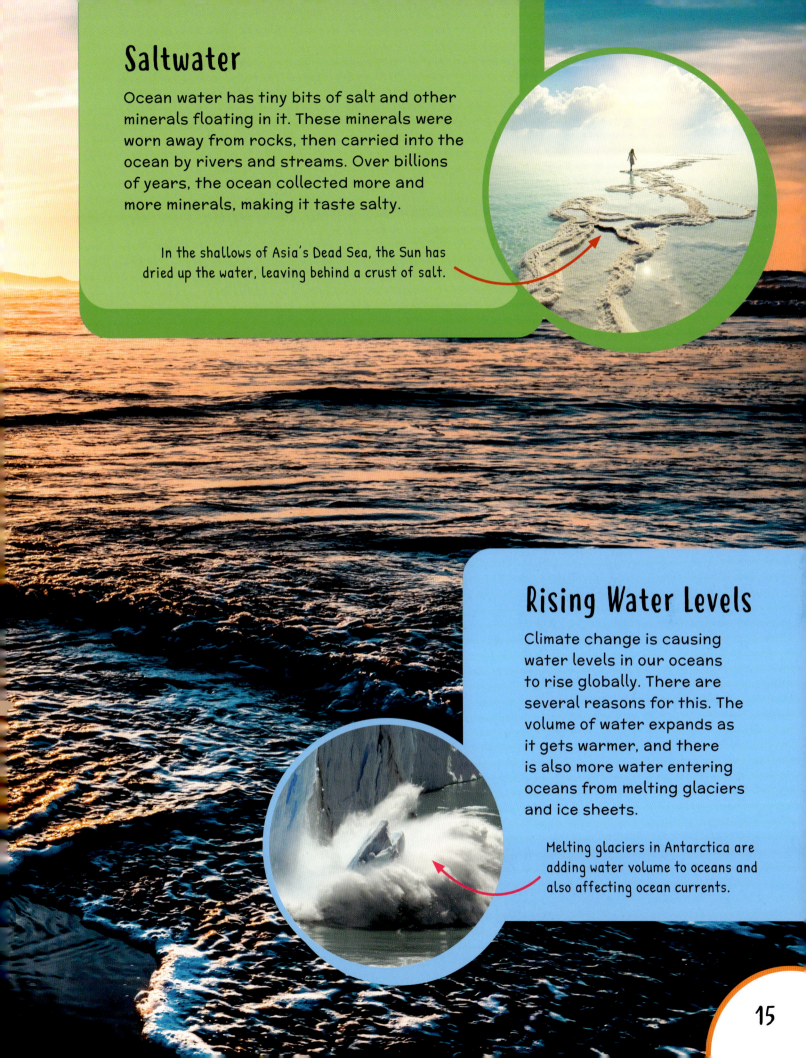

Saltwater

Ocean water has tiny bits of salt and other minerals floating in it. These minerals were worn away from rocks, then carried into the ocean by rivers and streams. Over billions of years, the ocean collected more and more minerals, making it taste salty.

In the shallows of Asia's Dead Sea, the Sun has dried up the water, leaving behind a crust of salt.

Rising Water Levels

Climate change is causing water levels in our oceans to rise globally. There are several reasons for this. The volume of water expands as it gets warmer, and there is also more water entering oceans from melting glaciers and ice sheets.

Melting glaciers in Antarctica are adding water volume to oceans and also affecting ocean currents.

15

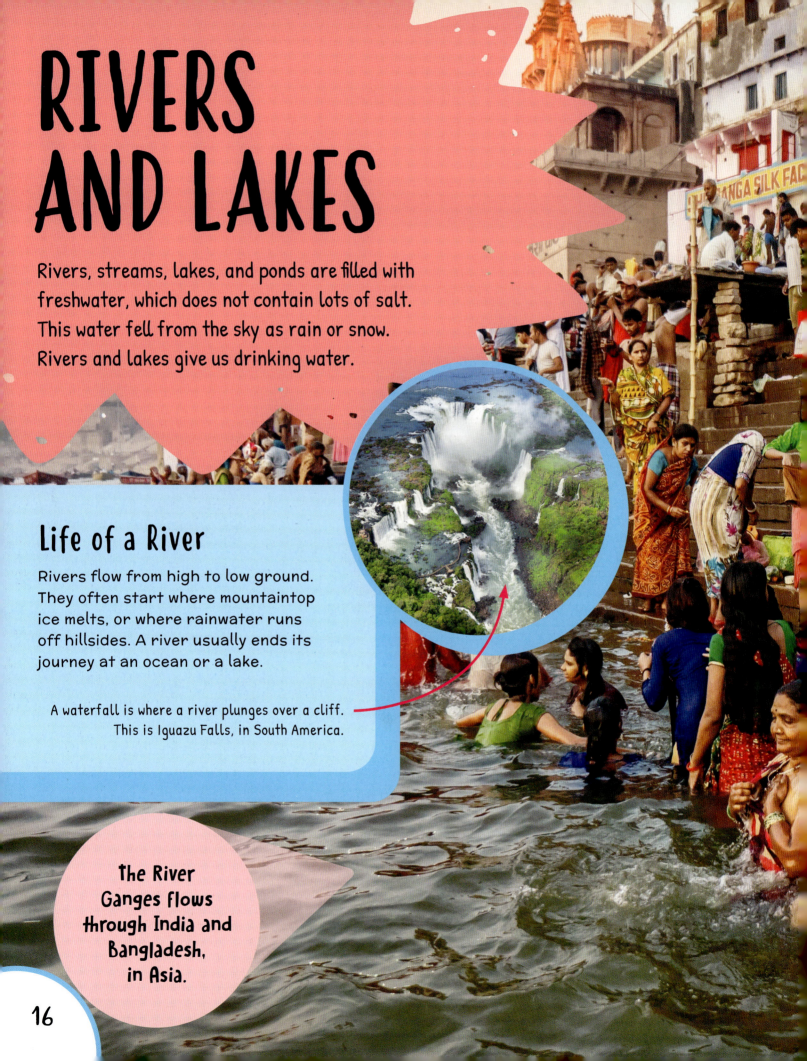

RIVERS AND LAKES

Rivers, streams, lakes, and ponds are filled with freshwater, which does not contain lots of salt. This water fell from the sky as rain or snow. Rivers and lakes give us drinking water.

Life of a River

Rivers flow from high to low ground. They often start where mountaintop ice melts, or where rainwater runs off hillsides. A river usually ends its journey at an ocean or a lake.

A waterfall is where a river plunges over a cliff. This is Iguazu Falls, in South America.

The River Ganges flows through India and Bangladesh, in Asia.

16

How Lakes Are Made

Lakes are hollows that are filled by rainwater, a river, melted ice, or water that has bubbled up from underground. Water bubbles up at a spring, where lots of rainwater has soaked into the ground.

A lake can form where a large mass of ice, called a glacier, is melting.

Hindus believe that the river cleans the soul as well as the body.

LONGEST RIVER

LENGTH: 6,695 km (4,160 miles) long
NAME: River Nile
WHERE: East Africa, from Burundi to the Mediterranean Sea on the coast of Egypt

RIVER NILE

MOUNTAINS

Mountains are areas of land that rise high and steeply above the surrounding land. Most mountains are part of mountain ranges, where many mountains are grouped in a line. Mountains are made by the movement of Earth's tectonic plates.

The highest mountain outside Asia is Aconcagua in Argentina, which is 6,960 m (22,837 ft) tall.

ROCK FOLDS

PLATES MOVE TOGETHER

Making Mountains

Mountains are usually made where two tectonic plates are moving toward each other. As one plate sinks below the other, rock is pushed and folded upward. Over millions of years, a mountain range grows.

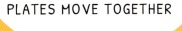

Rock folds into mountains, like a crumpled piece of paper.

Aconcagua is in the Andes mountain range, in South America.

LONGEST MOUNTAIN RANGE
LENGTH: 16,000 km (10,000 miles)
NAME: Mid-Atlantic Ridge
WHERE: Under the Atlantic Ocean

MID-ATLANTIC RIDGE

Still Growing

The Himalayas, in Asia, is the highest mountain range, reaching 8,848 m (29,029 ft) at Mount Everest. The range began to rise around 50 million years ago and is still growing, by 1 cm (2.5 in) a year.

Nanga Parbat is one of the Himalayas' youngest mountains, around 2 million years old.

EARTHQUAKES

Earthquakes are caused by the movement of Earth's tectonic plates. Most earthquakes happen at the edges of plates. In an earthquake, the ground shakes and may even crack.

How Earthquakes Happen

Earthquakes happen when plates are moving past each other, but get stuck because their edges are jagged. The rock suddenly cracks. This causes juddering that travels through the ground in waves, known as shock waves.

Shock waves travel through rock like ripples in bath water.

STRONGEST EARTHQUAKE
STRENGTH: Shock waves strong enough to travel across the world
WHERE: Valdivia, Chile
WHEN: May 22, 1960

VALDIVIA

A seismologist is burying a seismometer in the ground.

Taking Measurements

Scientists who study earthquakes are called seismologists. They use machines called seismometers to measure shock waves. They try to warn people if a big earthquake could be on its way.

A seismologist is studying the size of shock waves on his computer screen.

Information from the seismometer will be sent to the office via the internet.

21

TSUNAMIS

A tsunami is a giant wave that is very dangerous when it floods land beside the coast. Tsunamis can be set off by an undersea earthquake. Luckily, tsunamis do not happen often.

In 2011, a tsunami 40 m (133 ft) high flooded the Japanese coast.

How Tsunamis Start

If an earthquake lifts or drops the ocean floor, the water above rises up. Large waves spread across the ocean. The biggest waves can flood coasts thousands of miles away.

WATER RISES   TSUNAMI

EARTHQUAKE

An earthquake can start a series of giant waves that hit land one after another.

Escaping a Tsunami

When there is an earthquake that could set off a tsunami, warning sirens tell people to leave beaches and seaside towns. People climb to high ground quickly but carefully. Another warning sign that a tsunami is on its way is if the sea suddenly rises very high on the beach, or draws out a very long way.

In areas where tsunamis can happen, signs point the way to high ground.

TSUNAMI EVACUATION ROUTE

300 m.

The wave smashed and washed away weak buildings.

HIGHEST TSUNAMI
HEIGHT OF WAVES: 524 m (1,720 ft)
WHERE: Lituya Bay, Alaska, United States
WHEN: July 10, 1958

LITUYA BAY

VOLCANOES

Volcanoes are holes in Earth's crust where melted rock, called magma, can escape. Most volcanoes are on the edges of Earth's plates, where magma rises to the surface. This happens when tectonic plates are moving apart, or when they are pressing together, which melts lots of rock into magma.

At 3,776 m (12,389 ft), Mount Fuji is Japan's highest volcano.

Parts of a Volcano

Beneath a volcano is a pool of magma called a magma chamber. The magma can rise to the surface through a pipe called a conduit, reaching the surface at a vent. The vent may be in a bowl-shaped dip called a crater. Once magma has reached the surface, it is called lava.

Some volcanoes have more than one vent.

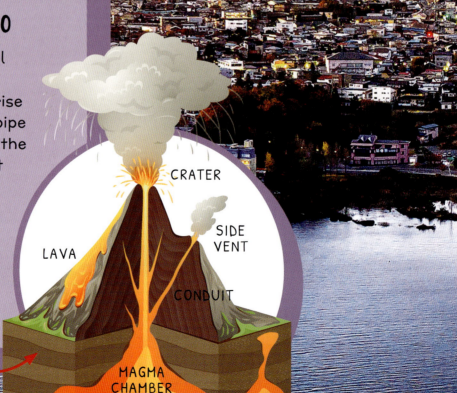

CRATER

SIDE VENT

LAVA

CONDUIT

MAGMA CHAMBER

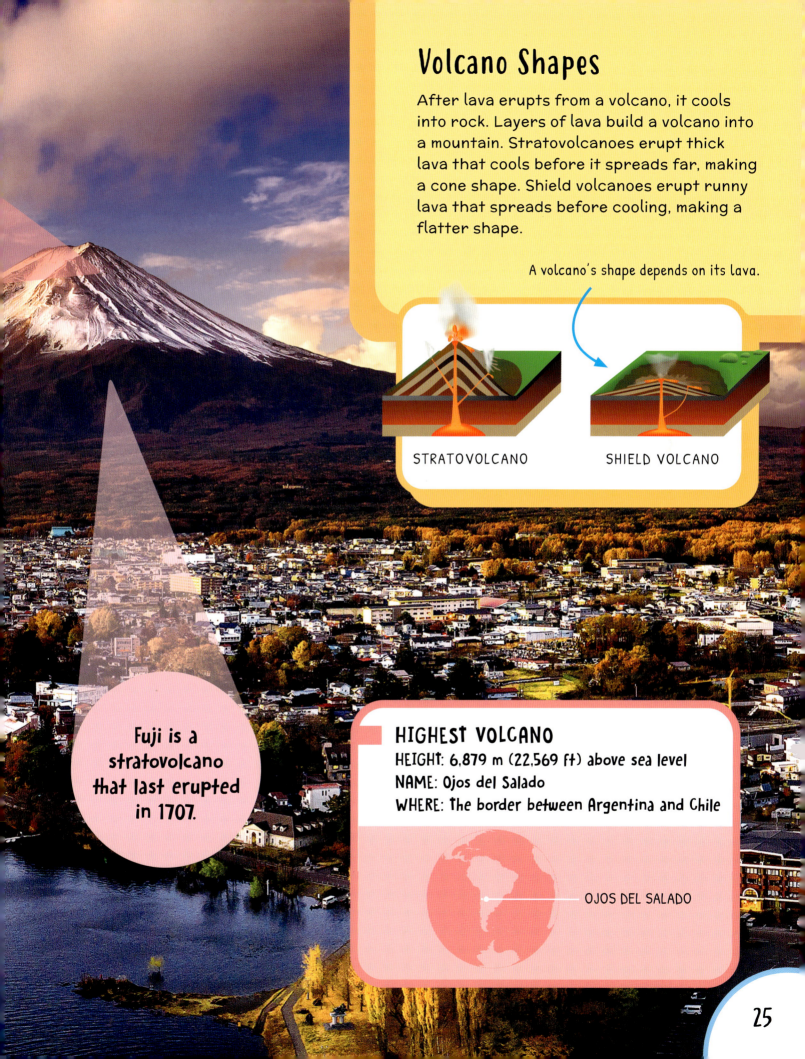

Volcano Shapes

After lava erupts from a volcano, it cools into rock. Layers of lava build a volcano into a mountain. Stratovolcanoes erupt thick lava that cools before it spreads far, making a cone shape. Shield volcanoes erupt runny lava that spreads before cooling, making a flatter shape.

A volcano's shape depends on its lava.

STRATOVOLCANO

SHIELD VOLCANO

Fuji is a stratovolcano that last erupted in 1707.

HIGHEST VOLCANO
HEIGHT: 6,879 m (22,569 ft) above sea level
NAME: Ojos del Salado
WHERE: the border between Argentina and Chile

OJOS DEL SALADO

25

WEATHER

The weather is what is happening in the air around Earth. It may be hot or cold, wet or dry, windy or calm. Weather is made by the heat of the Sun—which warms the land —water, and air. Weather is important to Earth's living things, as we need just the right amount of rain and warmth.

Different Weather

The weather can change from one hour to the next. It is different all over the world. There may be precipitation, which falls from the sky: hail, snow, or rain. The temperature, which is a measure of how hot it is, may be high or low.

Hail is a type of precipitation. These lumps of ice are made in thunderclouds.

During a rain shower, drops of water fall from clouds.

BIGGEST HAILSTONES
WIDTH: 20 cm (7.9 in)
WHERE: South Dakota, United States
WHEN: July 23, 2010

SOUTH DAKOTA

A rainbow is seen when drops of water split light into the spectrum, which we see as red, orange, yellow, green, blue, indigo, and violet.

Weather Matters

Most people hope for sunny days, but some people depend on the weather. Farmers need enough rain and sunshine to grow their crops. Sailors watch out for storms, while skiers hope for snow.

Rice plants needs plenty of rain and hot weather to grow well.

CLIMATE

Climate is the usual sort of weather in an area, year after year. A desert has a dry climate, while mountains have a cold, windy climate. Climate depends on how close a place is to the equator, how high it is, and if it is near the ocean.

HOTTEST PLACE
HIGHEST TEMPERATURE: 57 °C (134 °F)
WHERE: Death Valley, Mojave Desert, United States
WHEN: July 10, 1913

DEATH VALLEY

The Sahara Desert is in an area where the hot, dry air does not bring rain.

The Sun's Heat

The Sun does not heat everywhere on Earth equally. At the equator, the Sun's rays hit Earth straight on, making it hot. At the North and South Poles, however, the Sun's rays hit Earth at an angle, so they give much less warmth.

Near the poles, the Sun never rises high in the sky.

Climate Change

When humans burn fuels like coal and oil, we release carbon dioxide and other gases into the air. These trap the Sun's heat, making Earth warmer. This is changing climates, making places hotter, drier, or stormier.

With hotter, drier weather, wildfires are becoming more common.

A desert gets less than 25 cm (10 in) of rain in a year.

SEASONS

In most places, the weather changes through the year, creating seasons. Seasons are caused by the fact that Earth is slightly tilted as it makes it year-long journey around the Sun.

Tilting to the Sun

When the North Pole is tilted toward the Sun, the northern hemisphere gets most heat, giving it summer. When the North Pole is tilted away from the Sun, the northern hemisphere is coldest, giving it winter. Between those times, there is spring and fall or autumn.

When the northern hemisphere has winter, the southern hemisphere has summer.

In places with cold winters, many trees drop their leaves in fall or autumn.

KEY:
1. Winter in the northern hemisphere
2. Summer in the northern hemisphere

How Many Seasons?

Around the equator, Earth's tilt makes no difference to temperature. Some places there have no seasons. Others have two seasons: dry or rainy. Farther from the equator, there are four seasons: spring, summer, fall or autumn, and winter.

In India, the rainy season often brings floods.

MOST EXTREME SEASONS
RANGE: –68 °C (–90 °F) in winter; 37 °C (98 °F) in summer
WHERE: Verkhoyansk, Russia

VERKHOYANSK

Wide leaves would be damaged by cold, so trees take food from their leaves, then drop them.

THE ATMOSPHERE

The atmosphere is the blanket of gases, called air, that surrounds Earth. Nearly all weather happens in the layer of atmosphere closest to Earth. Without the atmosphere, there would be no life on Earth.

These climbers carry tanks of oxygen, breathing the gas through masks.

HIGHEST TOWN
HEIGHT: 5,130 m (16,830 ft)
NAME: La Rinconada
WHERE: Peru

LA RINCONADA

Over 8 km (5 miles) high on Mount Everest, the air is too thin to breathe easily.

Air and Water

Animals and plants need air to survive. Animals breathe the oxygen in air, while plants use the carbon dioxide and oxygen. Animals and plants also need water. The air contains lots of water vapor, which is water in the form of a gas.

Plants and animals need air, water, and sunlight.

KEY:

1. EXOSPHERE
Up to 10,000 km (6,200 miles).
Satellites orbit here.

2. THERMOSPHERE
Up to 700 km (440 miles).
The Sun's energy makes dancing lights over the poles.

3. MESOSPHERE
Up to 80 km (50 miles).
Rocks from space, called meteors, burn up here.

4. STRATOSPHERE
Up to 50 km (30 miles).
This layer is cold and very windy.

5. TROPOSPHERE
Up to 11 km (7 miles).
This is the layer where most of our weather happens.

Layers

The atmosphere is held around Earth by our planet's gravity. Moving up through the atmosphere, the air gets thinner. Out in space, there is no air at all.

WIND

Wind is the movement of air. Wind is useful to sailors, as well as plants that spread their seeds through the air. Fast winds, called gales or storms, can be dangerous when they whip up high waves or blow down trees and power lines.

Wind fills the sail of a yacht, pushing it across the water.

WINDIEST PLACE
WIND SPEED: Often over 240 km/h (150 miles per hour)
WHERE: Commonwealth Bay, Antarctica

COMMONWEALTH BAY

Warm Air Rises

When air is warmed by the Sun, it expands. This makes it lighter, so it rises. Cooler air rushes in to fill the space left by the warm air. We feel this movement as wind. Sometimes the movement is a gentle breeze. At other times, big differences in temperature make fast winds.

The Sun's heat creates winds.

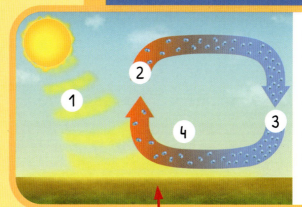

KEY:
1. The Sun warms the air.
2. Warm air rises, then cools.
3. Cool air sinks.
4. Air rushes to fill the space.

Wind Patterns

The Sun heats the equator more than the poles. This sets off air movements around the planet. Some winds are made by differences in temperature over land and sea, or over mountains and valleys.

This tree is bent over because the wind always blows from the sea.

When the wind is blowing the wrong way, extra sails help a yacht zigzag to its target.

CLOUDS

The air is full of water vapor. We cannot see this invisible gas. When the air cools, water vapor turns into liquid water. Then we can see millions of tiny drops of water floating in the air—as a cloud.

CLOUDIEST PLACE
HOURS OF SUNSHINE: **3 hours per day**, on average
WHERE: **Chengdu, China**

CHENGDU

White, puffy low clouds are called cumulus clouds.

Changing Water

When the Sun heats lakes and oceans, some water on the surface changes into water vapor. The water vapor rises in the warm air. As the air rises, it cools. Cold air cannot hold as much water vapor as warm air, so some water vapor turns into water drops.

KEY:
1. Water evaporates: It changes from liquid water into water vapor.
2. Water vapor rises.
3. Water vapor condenses: It changes into drops of liquid water.

The water drops in a cloud are so light they float in the air.

Cloud Types

Different types of clouds form at different heights and in different shapes. When the air is very full of water vapor, cloud can even form at ground level. This is called fog or mist.

Altocumulus clouds form at 2,000–6,100 m (6,600–20,000 ft).

Cirrus clouds form above 6,000 m (20,000 ft).

RAIN

If the water drops in a cloud grow too big and heavy, they will fall. As its water drops grow, a cloud changes from white to gray. This is a warning that it is time to find an umbrella.

RAINIEST PLACE
RAINFALL: 11.87 m (38.9 ft) per year, most of it during the rainy season
WHERE: Mawsynram, India

MAWSYNRAM

Rain and More Rain

Rain is often caused by a mass of warm air meeting a mass of cold air. The water vapor in the warm air cools, turning into low gray cloud that covers the sky. This brings rain that can last for days.

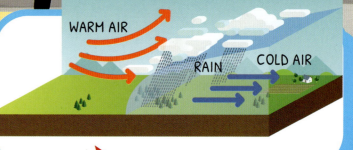

WARM AIR

RAIN

COLD AIR

When it meets cold air, a mass of warm air rises, making thick cloud.

SNOW

When it is very cold, a cloud's water drops freeze into ice crystals. If the ice crystals start to grow and stick together, they make snowflakes. When snowflakes get heavy enough, they fall to the ground.

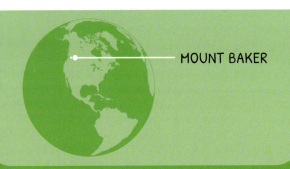
Snowflakes

When ice crystals join together into a snowflake, they make patterns. Snowflakes usually have six sides or points, but it is unlikely that two snowflakes will look completely the same.

A snowflake is never exactly symmetrical because its sides do not match.

THUNDERSTORMS

In a thunderstorm, sparks of electricity are made in huge clouds. The sparks create shock waves in the air, which we hear as thunder. Thunderstorms can also bring fast winds, heavy rain, and hail.

MOST LIGHTNING
LIGHTNING: 250 flashes per 1 sq km (0.4 sq miles) in a year
WHERE: Over the Catatumbo River, Venezuela

CATATUMBO RIVER

Towering Clouds

Thunderstorms happen in tall clouds called cumulonimbus clouds. They can be over 20 km (12 miles) high. These clouds form in very hot, wet air that rises fast. They can grow by the end of a hot day.

Thunderclouds are wider at the top than the bottom.

We hear thunder after we see lightning because light travels faster than sound.

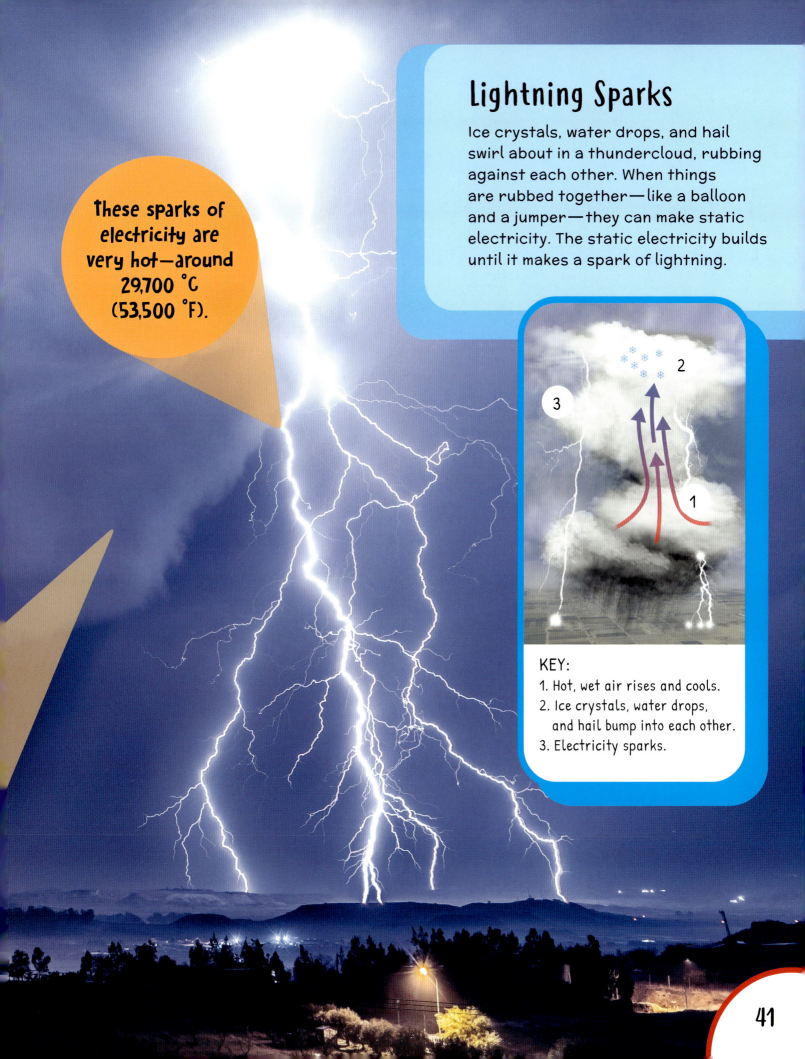

these sparks of electricity are very hot—around 29,700 °C (53,500 °F).

Lightning Sparks

Ice crystals, water drops, and hail swirl about in a thundercloud, rubbing against each other. When things are rubbed together—like a balloon and a jumper—they can make static electricity. The static electricity builds until it makes a spark of lightning.

KEY:
1. Hot, wet air rises and cools.
2. Ice crystals, water drops, and hail bump into each other.
3. Electricity sparks.

TORNADOES

Tornadoes are quickly spinning funnels of air. They are also called twisters. Tornadoes usually form in giant thunderclouds. The fastest tornadoes can suck up trees, cars, and even houses.

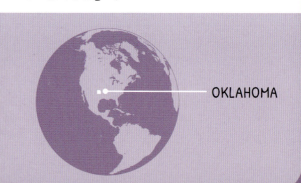

SWIRLING THUNDERCLOUD

RISING HOT AIR

Making a Tornado

Tornadoes grow inside thunderclouds when fast winds make the air swirl around. Hot air rises from the ground, joining the swirling air. The funnel of rising air spins quicker and quicker.

This tornado is moving in the direction of the red arrow, leaving a trail of damage behind.

HURRICANES

Hurricanes are giant, spinning storms. They start over warm oceans near the equator, but can then travel over land. Hurricanes have different names around the world, such as typhoons or cyclones.

FASTEST HURRICANE
WIND SPEED: 345 km/h (215 miles per hour)
NAME: Hurricane Patricia (named by weather scientists)
WHEN: October 20-24, 2015

HURRICANE PATRICIA'S PATH

Growing Storm

A hurricane starts when hot, wet air rises from the ocean. It forms tall storm clouds. Cool air rushes in to fill the space left by the rising air. As this air joins the storm, it starts to spin around and around. At the middle of the hurricane is a calmer, cloudless "eye."

Hurricanes can be up to 1,600 km (1,000 miles) wide.

HABITATS

An animal's or plant's habitat is its natural home, where it can find everything it needs to live. Some animals need a hot, dry habitat like the desert. Others live in grasslands or woods. Earth's habitats may be as large as a rain forest, or as small as a puddle.

The ibex lives in a mountain habitat, where it is rocky and cold.

A Suitable Home

A habitat has the right conditions for the living things that are found there. Each habitat's animals and plants are suited to the amount of light, heat, and water provided there, and they can find the food they need.

A rotting log is the perfect habitat for these termites.

World of Habitats

A region's main habitats depend on its climate. Climate is an area's usual weather. There are lots of types of major habitat, including:

1. POLAR ICE: See page 64
2. TUNDRA: See page 62
3. CONIFEROUS FOREST: See page 54
4. GRASSLAND OR WOODS: See pages 52 and 54
5. HOT DESERT: See page 48
6. RAIN FOREST: See page 50
7. OCEAN: See page 46

Only the toughest plants can make their home on high rock ledges.

OCEANS

Oceans have many different habitats, from beaches and seafloors, to coral reefs. In each habitat, the living things are dependent on each other. Plants may be eaten by small fish, which are eaten by big fish, birds, or whales.

In the Light

Sunlight reaches into the ocean's surface waters. Ocean plants use the Sun's energy to make food energy. These food-rich waters are busy with animals. They are all suited to warm, light waters.

In shallow water near the coast, seagrass is food for green turtles.

Coral reefs grow in warm, sunlit, shallow water.

LARGEST CORAL REEF
LENGTH: 2,300 km (1,400 miles)
NAME: Great Barrier Reef
WHERE: Off the northeast coast of Australia

GREAT BARRIER REEF

Crown butterflyfish eat coral and little worms.

In the Dark

In the deep, dark ocean, there are no plants. Fewer animals make their home here. Some fish have large eyes so they can see in what little light there is. Some make their own light in special body parts.

Günther's boafish has a glowing "lure" on its chin, attracting smaller fish for it to eat.

HOT DESERTS

A desert is a habitat with so little rain that few plants and animals can survive. Many deserts are in hot regions, which gives living things an extra challenge: keeping cool.

The fennec fox loses heat from its huge ears, helping it to stay cool.

Thick fur protects its feet from the hot sand.

Living With Heat

Many desert animals are nocturnal, which means they look for food at night. Rattlesnakes rest in the shade during the day, then come out at dusk. Kangaroo rats burrow underground, where it is cool.

The Cape ground squirrel uses its bushy tail as a sunshade to stay cool.

LARGEST HOT DESERT

AREA: 9.2 million sq km (3.5 million sq miles)
NAME: Sahara Desert
WHERE: Morocco to Egypt

SAHARA DESERT

Living Without Water

Animals need water, as it carries food through their bodies. Desert animals can live on the water they get from juicy plants or the blood of their prey. Some creatures, like scorpions, have a thick covering that saves water by stopping it from leaving their bodies.

The thorny devil lizard has scales with special ridges that collect water drops.

RAIN FORESTS

Tropical rain forests are found around the equator, in the region called the tropics. Here, it is hot and rainy all year round. Lots of sunlight and water makes trees grow tall, while shrubs and creepers live between and around their trunks.

Most trees keep their leaves all year, as it never gets cold.

LARGEST RAIN FOREST
AREA: 5.5 million sq km (2.1 million sq miles)
NAME: Amazon Rain Forest
WHERE: Colombia to Brazil

AMAZON RAIN FOREST

Scarlet macaws eat fruit, nuts, seeds, and insects.

In the Trees

Leaves, twigs, fruit, and nuts offer food for insects, birds, monkeys, and many other animals. Animals that live above the ground must crawl, fly, or swing around.

The tail of a howler monkey can curl tight around branches.

On the Forest Floor

The forest floor is dark and damp. Rotting leaves are food for mushrooms. Tarantulas hunt for insects and mice. Amphibians, such as frogs and toads, find the water they need to survive.

With its rough brown skin, the sharp-nosed toad is well camouflaged among the fallen leaves.

51

GRASSLANDS

Grasslands are areas where most plants are grasses. Larger plants and trees have not been able to grow because of little rainfall, frequent wildfires, or the constant nibbling of plant-eating animals.

Steppe and Prairie

Grassland is common in temperate regions, which lie between the cold poles and the hot tropics. In northern Asia, the grasslands are called steppe. In North America, they are called prairie.

When it is too cold or dry, prairie dogs rest inside their burrow.

Herds of zebras graze the grasses of the African savanna.

Savanna

In the tropics, savanna is a common habitat. Here, grassland is dotted with shrubs and trees. Most rain falls in the yearly rainy season. Savanna animals often travel long distances to find water.

A herd of wildebeest crosses the savanna in search of water.

LARGEST GRASSLAND
AREA: 8.6 million sq km
(3.3 million sq miles)
NAME: Eurasian Steppe
WHERE: Hungary to China

EURASIAN STEPPE

Grasses are short plants with hollow stems and long, narrow leaves.

53

FORESTS AND WOODS

A forest is an area where many trees grow close together. In a wood, the trees are farther apart, so sunlight can reach the ground. Woods and forests are in places with enough rain to water these huge plants. The trees' leaves turn the Sun's energy into food energy.

The European roe deer lives in woods, eating leaves and berries.

LARGEST CONIFEROUS FOREST
AREA: 7.7 million sq km (3 million sq miles)
NAME: Eurasian taiga
WHERE: Sweden to Russia

EURASIAN TAIGA

Types of Trees

In temperate regions, where there are short but cold winters, many trees are deciduous. These trees drop their delicate leaves before winter. Farther north, most trees are coniferous. They have tough, needle-shaped leaves that stay on the tree through long, snowy winters.

Chestnut is a deciduous tree.

Norway spruce is a coniferous tree.

Oak, maple, and beech trees are common in deciduous woods.

Nesting in Trees

Most forest birds make nests in trees, where their eggs are safe from ground-living animals. Some build nests of twigs, while others use holes in trees.

These pileated woodpecker chicks are in a nest hole that their father drilled with his beak.

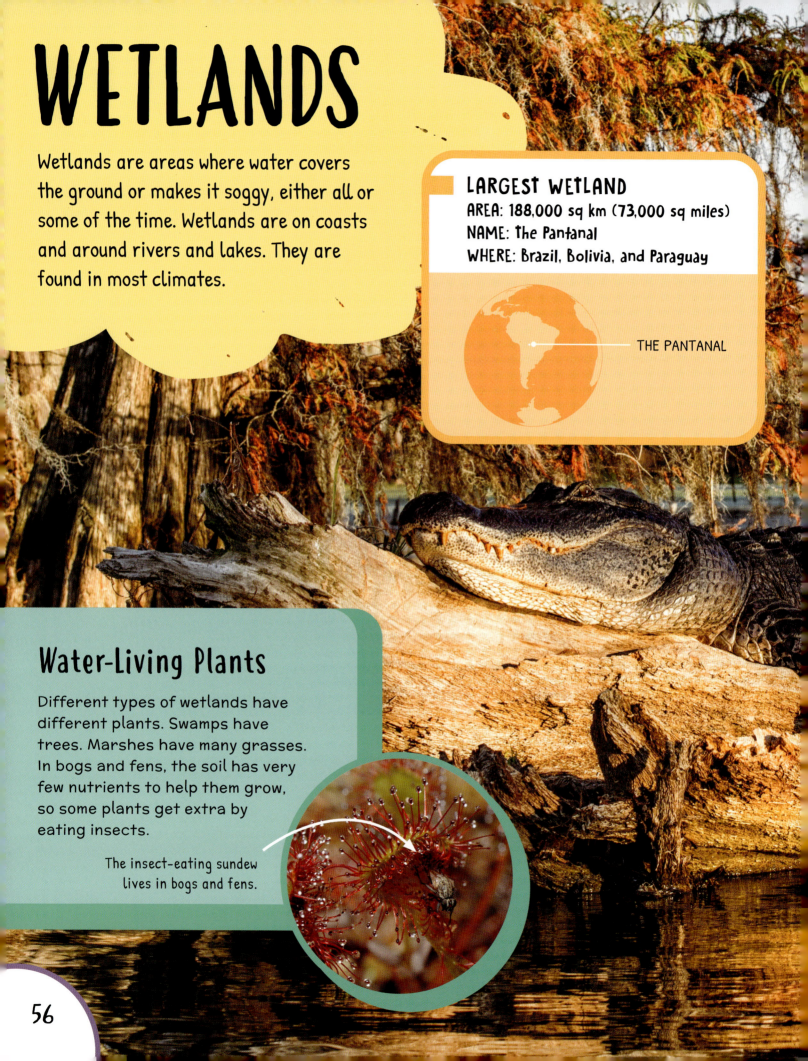

WETLANDS

Wetlands are areas where water covers the ground or makes it soggy, either all or some of the time. Wetlands are on coasts and around rivers and lakes. They are found in most climates.

LARGEST WETLAND
AREA: 188,000 sq km (73,000 sq miles)
NAME: the Pantanal
WHERE: Brazil, Bolivia, and Paraguay

THE PANTANAL

Water-Living Plants

Different types of wetlands have different plants. Swamps have trees. Marshes have many grasses. In bogs and fens, the soil has very few nutrients to help them grow, so some plants get extra by eating insects.

The insect-eating sundew lives in bogs and fens.

Between Two Worlds

Many wetland animals move between water and land. Insects like diving beetles can both swim and fly. Long-legged wading birds dip their beaks in the water for fish.

Lechwe have longer back legs to help them run through knee-deep water in Africa's wetlands.

Cypresses grow in the United States' Atchafalaya Swamp.

Alligators are suited to wetlands as they can both swim and walk.

FARMLAND

Farmland is a human-made habitat. More than one-third of Earth's land is used for farming. Some farms grow useful plants, called crops. Some farms keep animals, called livestock.

Growing Crops

Crops like rice and apples are grown for food. Some crops, like cotton and flax, are used to make cloth. Sunflowers and canola are made into cooking oil and even fuel for cars.

Bees visit sunflower fields to collect nectar and pollen.

LARGEST FARM
AREA: 90,000 sq km (35,000 sq miles)
NAME: Mudanjiang City Mega Farm
WHERE: Heilongjiang, China

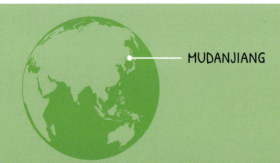

MUDANJIANG

Keeping Animals

Humans keep animals for their milk, meat, eggs, or wool. Thousands of years ago, people captured wild pigs, chickens, goats, and other animals that are kept on farms today.

These sheep are being moved to a field of fresh grass, under the care of a trained sheepdog.

White storks are sometimes seen on farms, eating insects in newly cut grass.

Tractors help farmers prepare the soil and harvest crops.

CITIES AND TOWNS

Around 8 billion people live on Earth. More than half of them live in cities and towns. People gather in cities and towns because they offer plenty of access to work, homes, schools, and places to shop.

Human Habitat

Humans have built cities as a habitat for themselves. Cities supply many of the things that humans need: supermarkets, hospitals, sports facilities, and the company of other people.

Cities are often overcrowded with people and traffic.

Nests are made on high cliffs, tall trees—or city balconies.

LARGEST CITY
NUMBER OF PEOPLE: 38 million
NAME: Tokyo
WHERE: Japan

TOKYO

The peregrine falcon is common in cities, where it hunts pigeons and ducks.

Side by Side

Over hundreds or thousands of years, some wild animals have adapted to living in cities. Foxes, rats, raccoons, and pigeons find food among the garbage that humans leave behind. Insects like cockroaches live in human homes.

A raccoon hunts for food in New York City.

TUNDRA

Tundra is found in Earth's far north, just to the south of the polar ice. In the tundra, snow covers the ground in winter, but melts in summer. However, the soil stays partly frozen all year.

In summer, the ground is often soggy as the snow melts.

Plant Life

There are no trees in the tundra, because their large roots cannot push down into the frozen soil. There are only small, tough plants such as grasses, mosses, and low shrubs.

Cloudberries can survive temperatures as low as -40 °C (-40 °F).

Musk oxen have extremely long, thick, warm hair.

Animal Life

Tundra animals have thick fur or feathers to stay warm. During the long, dark winter, many hibernate, resting in a warm den or burrow.

The Norway lemming spends the winter in a nest beneath the snow.

COUNTRY WITH MOST TUNDRA
AREA: 1.6 million sq km (600,000 sq miles)
NAME: Russia

RUSSIAN TUNDRA

THE POLES

The North Pole lies in the middle of the Arctic Ocean. It is so cold that much of the ocean is frozen over. The South Pole is on the continent of Antarctica. Nearly all of Antarctica is always covered by ice around 1.9 km (1.2 miles) thick.

No plants can grow on the ice of Antarctica.

Polar Animals

Few animals live on the polar ice. Animals that live close to the North Pole include polar bears, ringed seals, and seabirds such as northern fulmars. No animals live close to the South Pole, but seals, penguins, and a few other seabirds visit the coasts of Antarctica.

Polar bears spend most of their lives on the ice that covers the Arctic Ocean.

Food From the Sea

Most polar animals dive into the ocean to catch fish, squid, and other sea creatures. Polar bears hunt seals when they are resting on the ice, or when they come to the surface to breathe.

A bearded seal is about to dive into the Arctic Ocean in search of cod, clams, and squid.

Emperor penguins have a thick layer of fat to keep them warm.

COLDEST PLACE
TEMPERATURE: –89 °C (–128 °F)
WHERE: Vostok Research Station, Antarctica
WHEN: July 21, 1983

VOSTOK RESEARCH STATION

SPACE

We live on a small, rocky planet named Earth. Our planet is just one of 100 billion planets in our galaxy, and there are 100 billion galaxies in the Universe. The Universe is really huge! In fact, as far as we know, the Universe is everything that exists.

Sparkling Stars

From Earth, you can see about 500 stars at night, but astronomers know that there are many, many more. Stars are glowing balls of gas, which we can see in the night sky as twinkling lights.

Our nearest star, the Sun, is 15 million °C (27 million °F) at its core.

Astronaut Stephen Robinson spacewalks 400 km (250 miles) above Earth.

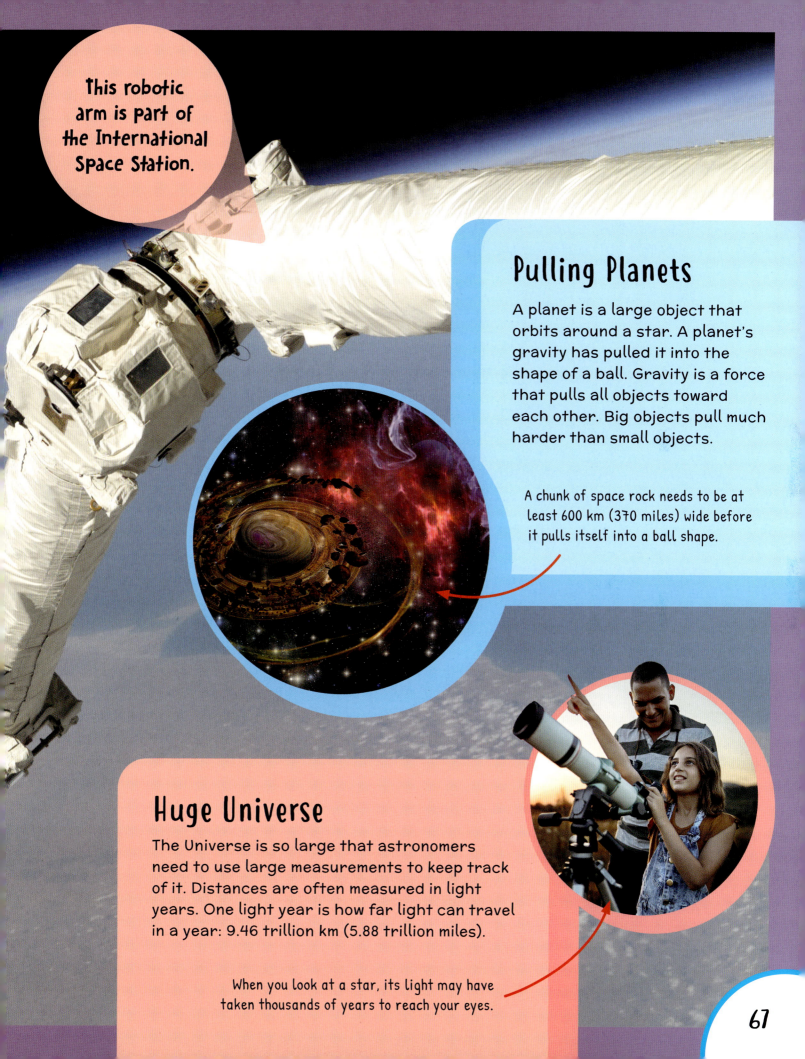

This robotic arm is part of the International Space Station.

Pulling Planets

A planet is a large object that orbits around a star. A planet's gravity has pulled it into the shape of a ball. Gravity is a force that pulls all objects toward each other. Big objects pull much harder than small objects.

A chunk of space rock needs to be at least 600 km (370 miles) wide before it pulls itself into a ball shape.

Huge Universe

The Universe is so large that astronomers need to use large measurements to keep track of it. Distances are often measured in light years. One light year is how far light can travel in a year: 9.46 trillion km (5.88 trillion miles).

When you look at a star, its light may have taken thousands of years to reach your eyes.

THE SOLAR SYSTEM

In the middle of our Solar System is a star named the Sun. This ball of hot gas gives us light and heat. The Solar System includes all the planets, moons, rocks, and ice that spin around the Sun.

JUPITER

ASTEROID BELT

SUN

MERCURY

VENUS

EARTH

MARS

The planets travel around the Sun on a curved path, named an orbit.

THE SOLAR SYSTEM
SIZE: 27 billion km
    (16.8 billion miles) across
DISTANCE FROM MIDDLE OF MILKY
    WAY GALAXY: 27,000 light years
KNOWN PLANETS: 8

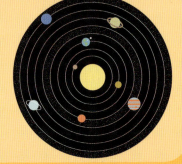

Birth of the Planets

Around 4.5 billion years ago, a cloud of gas and dust was spinning around the young Sun. Clumps formed in the cloud. As the clumps grew, their gravity pulled in more material—making planets.

It took millions of years for the planets to form.

SATURN

URANUS

NEPTUNE

The planets are held in orbit by the Sun's gravity.

KEY:
1. Solid metal inner core
2. Liquid metal outer core
3. Partly melted rock
4. Solid rock

Heavy or Light?

The four inner planets are made of heavier materials than the outer planets. Lighter materials were blown away from the Sun into the outer Solar System, where Jupiter, Saturn, Uranus, and Neptune formed.

KEY:
1. Rocky core
2. Metallic hydrogen
3. Liquid hydrogen
4. Hydrogen gas

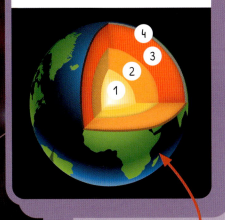

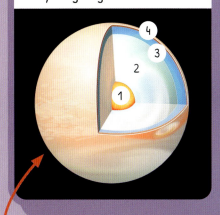

Earth and the other inner planets are made of metal and rock.

Jupiter and the other outer planets contain icy or gassy materials, such as hydrogen.

MERCURY

Mercury is the smallest of the Solar System's eight planets. It orbits closest to the Sun, giving it the shortest and fastest orbit. Mercury takes only 88 days to travel around the Sun, at a speed of 47 km (27 miles) per second.

These streaks are dust thrown out by a space rock crash.

Crashing Craters

Mercury's surface is covered in craters. These were made billions of years ago when space rocks, called comets, and asteroids crashed into the planet.

This photo shows the different heights of Mercury's surface in different shades, with purple for the lowest areas and red for the highest.

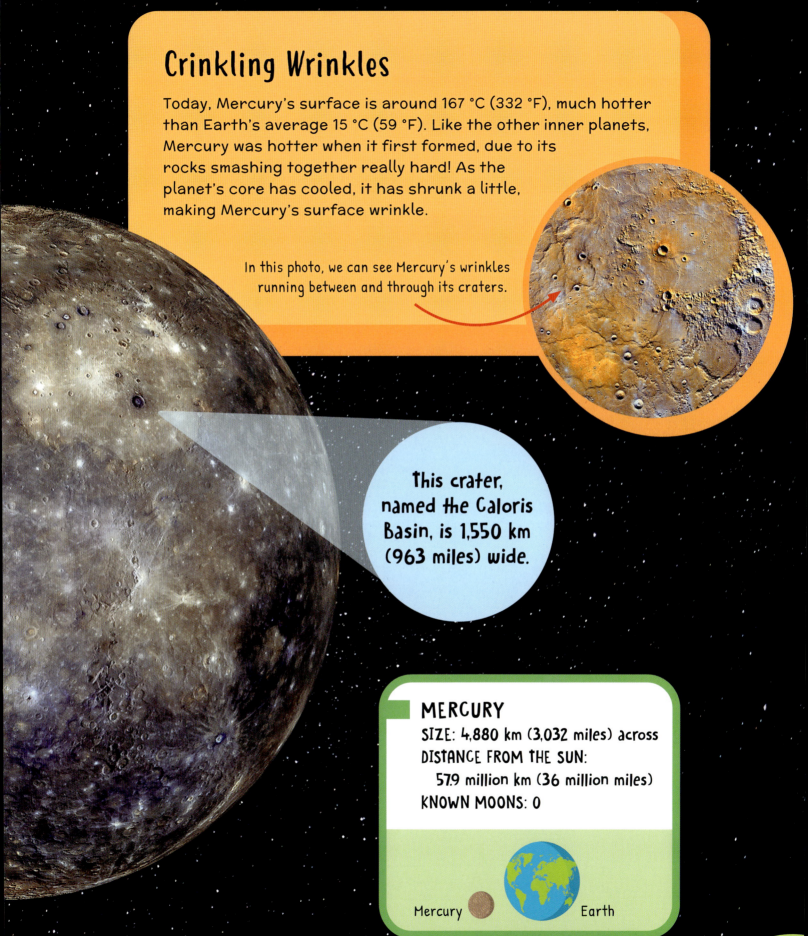

Crinkling Wrinkles

Today, Mercury's surface is around 167 °C (332 °F), much hotter than Earth's average 15 °C (59 °F). Like the other inner planets, Mercury was hotter when it first formed, due to its rocks smashing together really hard! As the planet's core has cooled, it has shrunk a little, making Mercury's surface wrinkle.

In this photo, we can see Mercury's wrinkles running between and through its craters.

This crater, named the Caloris Basin, is 1,550 km (963 miles) wide.

MERCURY
SIZE: 4,880 km (3,032 miles) across
DISTANCE FROM THE SUN:
   57.9 million km (36 million miles)
KNOWN MOONS: 0

Mercury   Earth

VENUS

Like all the planets, Venus turns around its own axis (a line through its middle) as it orbits the Sun. Venus has the slowest rotation of all the planets: One turn takes 243 days.

VENUS
SIZE: 12,104 km (7,521 miles) across
DISTANCE FROM THE SUN:
    108.2 million km (67.2 million miles)
KNOWN MOONS: 0

Venus

Earth

Dark areas are old, cooled lava flows.

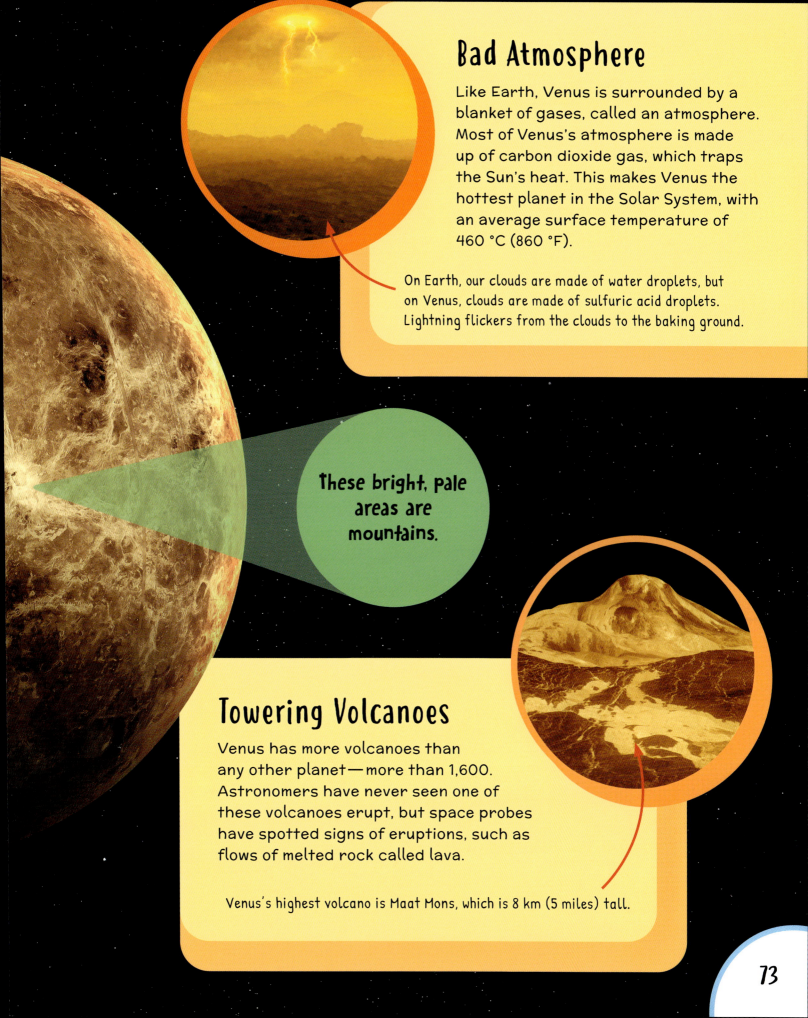

Bad Atmosphere

Like Earth, Venus is surrounded by a blanket of gases, called an atmosphere. Most of Venus's atmosphere is made up of carbon dioxide gas, which traps the Sun's heat. This makes Venus the hottest planet in the Solar System, with an average surface temperature of 460 °C (860 °F).

On Earth, our clouds are made of water droplets, but on Venus, clouds are made of sulfuric acid droplets. Lightning flickers from the clouds to the baking ground.

These bright, pale areas are mountains.

Towering Volcanoes

Venus has more volcanoes than any other planet—more than 1,600. Astronomers have never seen one of these volcanoes erupt, but space probes have spotted signs of eruptions, such as flows of melted rock called lava.

Venus's highest volcano is Maat Mons, which is 8 km (5 miles) tall.

EARTH

Earth is a special planet because it is the perfect distance from its star! At this distance, Earth is warm enough for its water to flow—rather than all freeze into ice or sizzle into steam. Without Earth's oceans, rivers, and rain, there would be no animals and plants!

This photo of Earth was taken from onboard *Apollo 8*.

Days and Years

Earth turns around its axis, making one rotation every 24 hours. When one side of Earth is facing the Sun, it has daylight. When that side faces away from the Sun, it has night. As well as rotating on its axis, Earth also travels around the Sun. It takes 365.25 days to make one orbit. Earth's axis is slightly tilted. When the northern half, or hemisphere, of Earth is tilted toward the Sun, it has summer. When the northern hemisphere is tilted away from the Sun, it has winter.

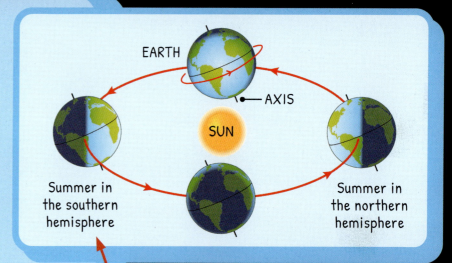

EARTH

AXIS

SUN

Summer in the southern hemisphere

Summer in the northern hemisphere

Summer brings warmer weather and longer days.

In 1968, *Apollo 8* was the first spacecraft to orbit the Moon.

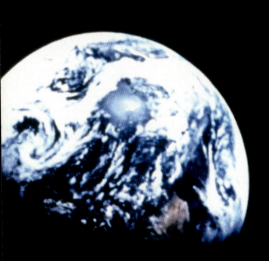

EARTH
SIZE: 12,742 km (7,918 miles) across
DISTANCE FROM THE SUN: 149.6 million km
  (93 million miles)
KNOWN MOONS: 1

Earth 🌍   Sun

Airy Atmosphere

Earth's gravity holds a mixture of gases, called air, around it. Air contains oxygen, which animals need in order to breathe. Scientists divide Earth's atmosphere into layers, each less tightly packed with air than the one below.

Many satellites orbit in the exosphere.

Particles from the Sun make lights known as auroras.

Small space rocks burn up here, making "shooting stars."

Planes soar among the clouds of the troposphere.

Weather balloons float here to measure conditions.

KEY:

1. Exosphere:
   10,000 km
   (6,200 miles)

2. Thermosphere:
   500 km (300 miles)

3. Mesosphere:
   80 km (50 miles)

4. Stratosphere:
   40 km (25 miles)

5. Troposphere:
   10 km (6 miles)

THE MOON

The Moon has been orbiting our planet since Earth was around 100 million years old. The dark areas we can see on the Moon, sometimes called "seas," are hardened lava that was spewed from volcanoes that erupted long ago.

THE MOON
SIZE: 3,476 km (2,160 miles) across
DISTANCE FROM EARTH: 384,402 km
  (238,856 miles)
ORBIT AROUND EARTH: 27 days

 Moon Earth

This crater, named Tycho, was made 108 million years ago.

The Sea of Serenity is 674 km (419 miles) wide.

Making the Moon

Most astronomers think the Moon was made when another planet crashed into the young Earth. The crash sent rock and metal shooting into space. Earth's gravity held this material in orbit, where it collected together, becoming the Moon.

Astronomers have named the planet that crashed into Earth: Theia.

THEIA

CRASH

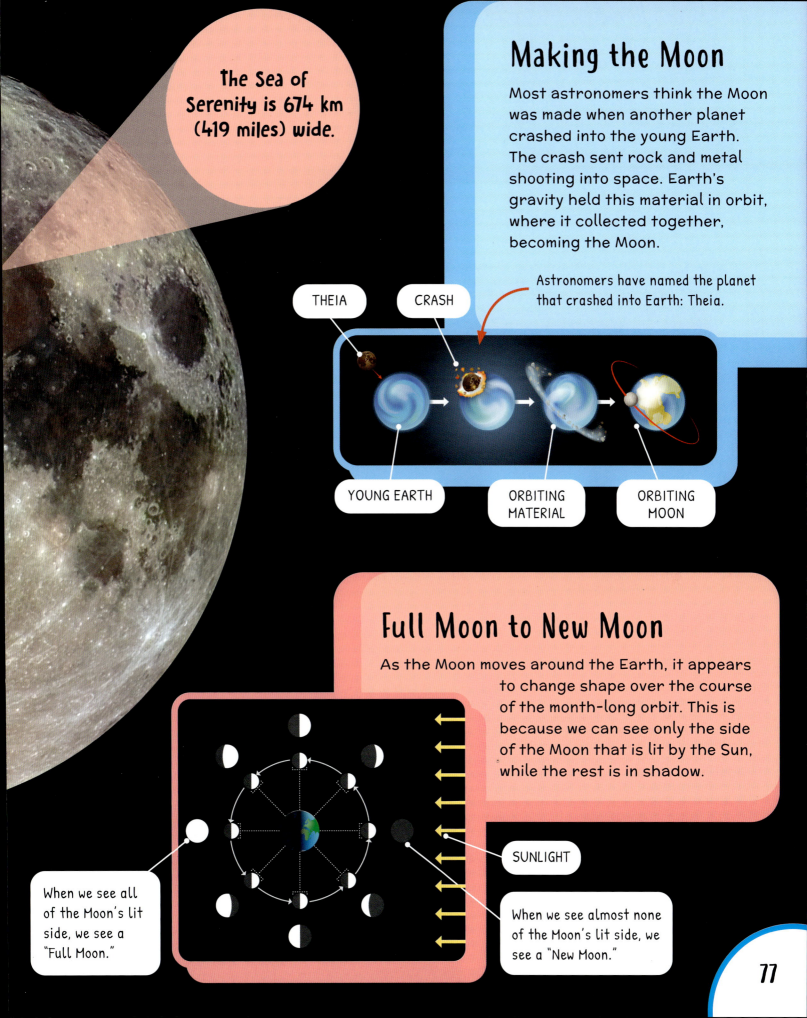

YOUNG EARTH

ORBITING MATERIAL

ORBITING MOON

Full Moon to New Moon

As the Moon moves around the Earth, it appears to change shape over the course of the month-long orbit. This is because we can see only the side of the Moon that is lit by the Sun, while the rest is in shadow.

SUNLIGHT

When we see all of the Moon's lit side, we see a "Full Moon."

When we see almost none of the Moon's lit side, we see a "New Moon."

MARS

Today, Mars is a dry and lifeless planet. But astronomers think the planet once had oceans like Earth's. They even wonder if—long ago—Mars might have been home to tiny living things.

the cold north pole is covered by ice.

Signs of Life?

Astronomers can see that some of Mars's rocks were worn away by waves and rivers. On Earth, the oceans were where life began, around 4 billion years ago. If Mars's oceans were home to living things, no sign of them has been found—so far!

The *Perseverance* rover took this photo on Mars. Mars's rocks are red and dusty because they contain iron, which can rust—turning red—like old metal.

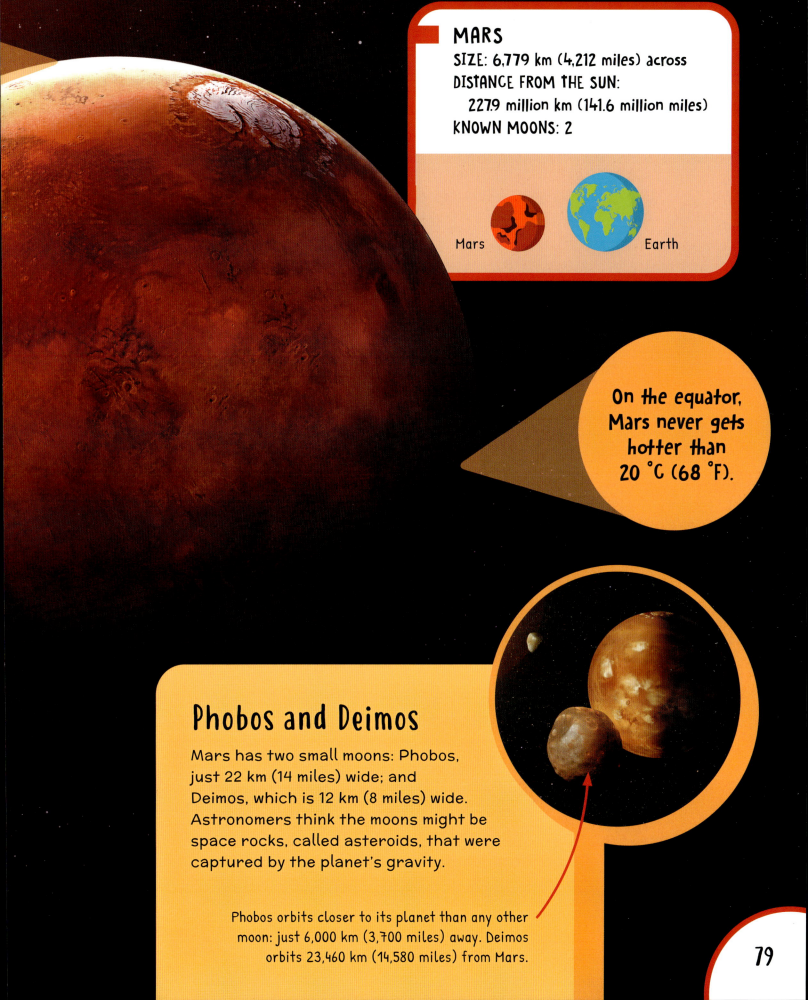

MARS
SIZE: 6,779 km (4,212 miles) across
DISTANCE FROM THE SUN:
  227.9 million km (141.6 million miles)
KNOWN MOONS: 2

Mars

Earth

On the equator, Mars never gets hotter than 20 °C (68 °F).

Phobos and Deimos

Mars has two small moons: Phobos, just 22 km (14 miles) wide; and Deimos, which is 12 km (8 miles) wide. Astronomers think the moons might be space rocks, called asteroids, that were captured by the planet's gravity.

Phobos orbits closer to its planet than any other moon: just 6,000 km (3,700 miles) away. Deimos orbits 23,460 km (14,580 miles) from Mars.

THE ASTEROID BELT

Asteroids are made of rock and metal. Millions of them are circling the Sun between the orbits of Mars and Jupiter. Most asteroids are tiny, but more than 1 million are wider than 1 km (0.6 miles).

Asteroid Attack!

Most asteroids orbit in the Asteroid Belt, but around 27,000 have orbits that cross Earth's. Astronomers watch these asteroids closely. If a big asteroid comes too near, they will fly a space probe into it—knocking the asteroid off course!

Scientists think an asteroid 10 km (6 miles) wide hit Earth 66 million years ago, creating fires and dust clouds that wiped out the dinosaurs.

Asteroids are bits of material left over from the formation of the planets.

the Asteroid Belt is 180 million km (112 million miles) wide.

Ceres the Dwarf Planet

The largest asteroid is named Ceres. Astronomers say Ceres is a dwarf planet. A dwarf planet is large enough for its gravity to pull it into a ball shape. Unlike a true planet, it is not large enough to clear other objects out of its orbit.

This photo of Ceres was taken by the *Dawn* space probe. We can see Ceres's bright crater, named Occator.

CERES

SIZE: 940 km (580 miles) across
DISTANCE FROM THE SUN:
   413.8 million km (257 million miles)
KNOWN MOONS: 0

Ceres   Earth

81

JUPITER

The Solar System's largest planet is mostly swirling hydrogen. In Jupiter's outer layers, the hydrogen is a gas but—deeper inside—it is pressed and heated into a flowing liquid. Like all the outer planets, Jupiter does not have a solid surface!

JUPITER
SIZE: 142,984 km (88,846 miles) across
DISTANCE FROM THE SUN:
    778.5 million km (483.7 million miles)
KNOWN MOONS: 79

Jupiter   🌍 Earth

Jupiter is rotating at 45,000 km/h (28,000 miles per hour).

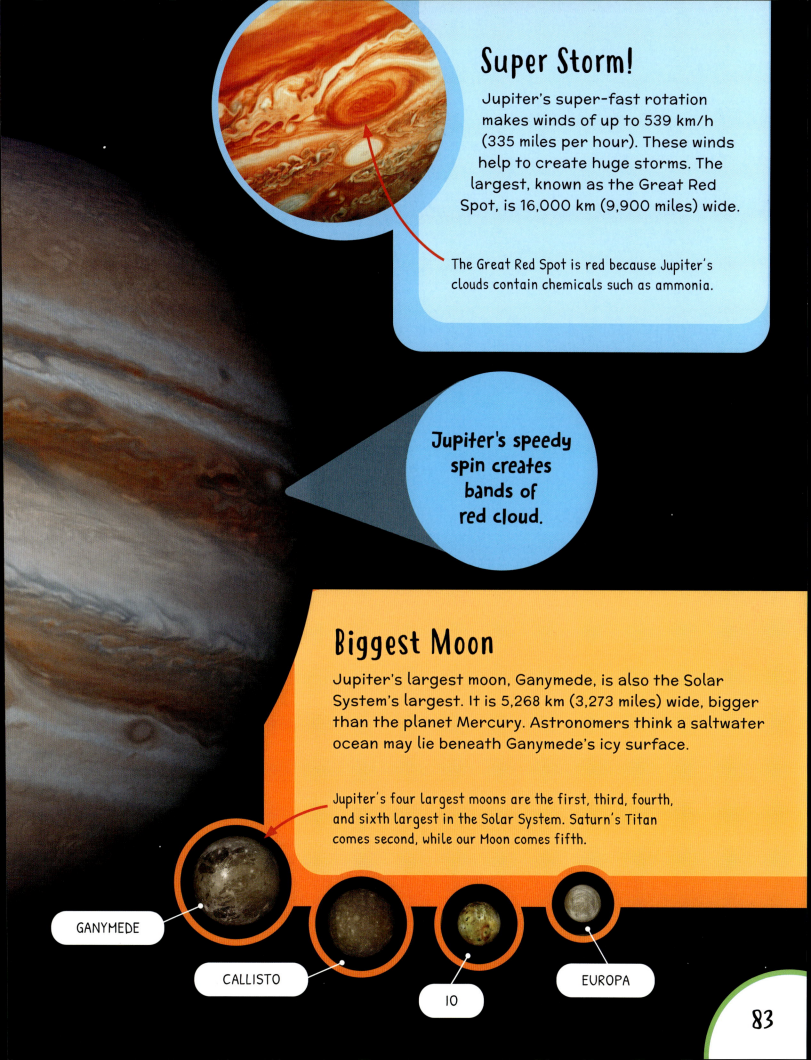

Super Storm!

Jupiter's super-fast rotation makes winds of up to 539 km/h (335 miles per hour). These winds help to create huge storms. The largest, known as the Great Red Spot, is 16,000 km (9,900 miles) wide.

The Great Red Spot is red because Jupiter's clouds contain chemicals such as ammonia.

Jupiter's speedy spin creates bands of red cloud.

Biggest Moon

Jupiter's largest moon, Ganymede, is also the Solar System's largest. It is 5,268 km (3,273 miles) wide, bigger than the planet Mercury. Astronomers think a saltwater ocean may lie beneath Ganymede's icy surface.

Jupiter's four largest moons are the first, third, fourth, and sixth largest in the Solar System. Saturn's Titan comes second, while our Moon comes fifth.

GANYMEDE

CALLISTO

IO

EUROPA

83

SATURN

Saturn is the most distant planet that we can see in the night sky without a telescope. Like the other planets—apart from Earth—it was named after a Greek or Roman god. Saturn was the Roman god of farming.

This gap between rings is named the Cassini Division.

Shining Rings

All four of the outer planets have rings, which are made of chunks of rock and ice. Saturn's rings are the largest and brightest, stretching up to 400,000 km (248,550 miles) from the planet's equator.

This image has been tinted, to show the size of the chunks in the rings. Purple areas contain chunks bigger than 5 cm (2 in) wide. Green areas contain smaller pieces.

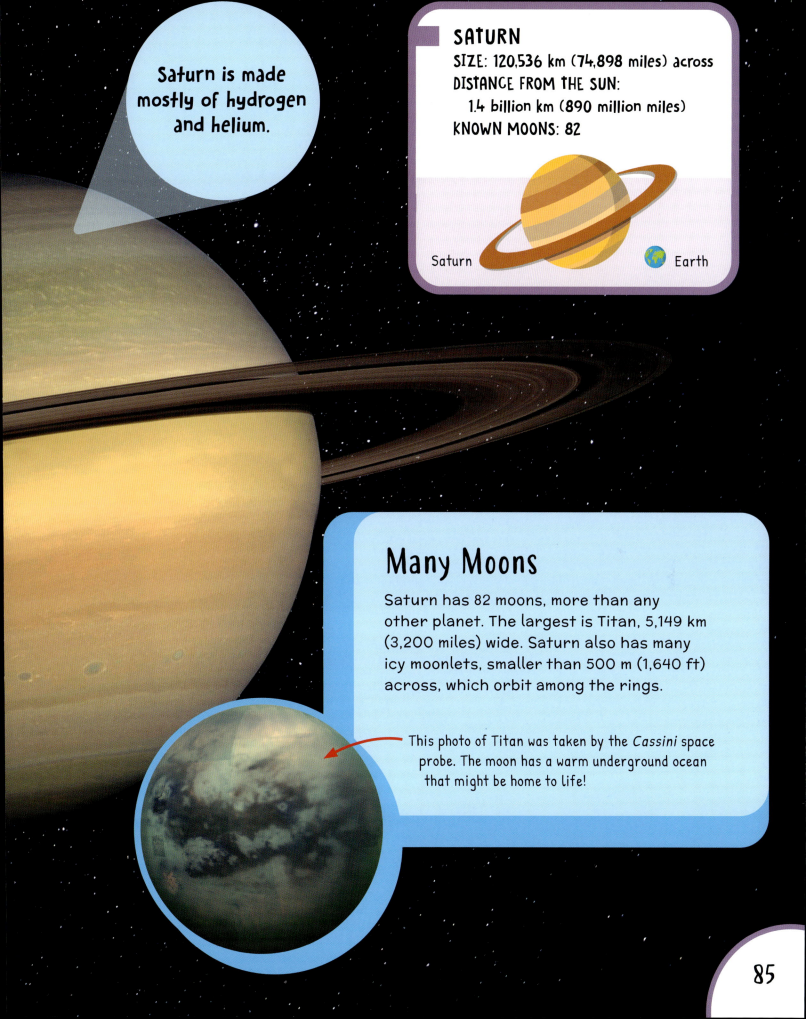

Saturn is made mostly of hydrogen and helium.

SATURN
SIZE: 120,536 km (74,898 miles) across
DISTANCE FROM THE SUN:
 1.4 billion km (890 million miles)
KNOWN MOONS: 82

Saturn

Earth

Many Moons

Saturn has 82 moons, more than any other planet. The largest is Titan, 5,149 km (3,200 miles) wide. Saturn also has many icy moonlets, smaller than 500 m (1,640 ft) across, which orbit among the rings.

This photo of Titan was taken by the *Cassini* space probe. The moon has a warm underground ocean that might be home to life!

URANUS

Uranus and Neptune are made mostly of three chemicals: water, ammonia, and methane. The methane makes Uranus look greenish blue. Although the planet's surface is cold, its rocky core reaches 5,000 °C (9,000 °F).

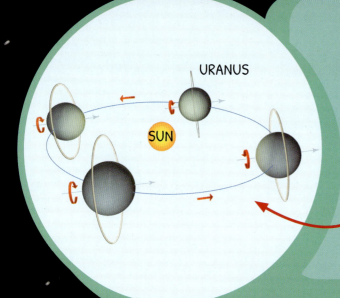

URANUS

SUN

Knocked Sideways

Unlike the other planets, Uranus orbits the Sun on its side, with its rings pointing upward. Astronomers think that, billions of years ago, Uranus was knocked sideways by a collision with another planet.

Uranus's orbit takes 84 years. The planet's north pole has 42 years of sunlight, followed by 42 years of darkness.

Cold Planet

Uranus is not the farthest planet from the Sun, but it is the coldest. Its surface reaches −224 °C (−371 °F), a few degrees colder than Neptune. This is also a result of Uranus's collision, which let out some of the heat trapped inside the planet.

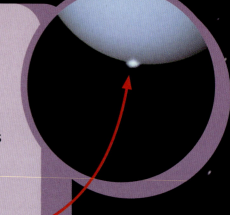

Lights, known as auroras, can be seen near Uranus's icy surface. They are made when gases are lit up by particles from the Sun.

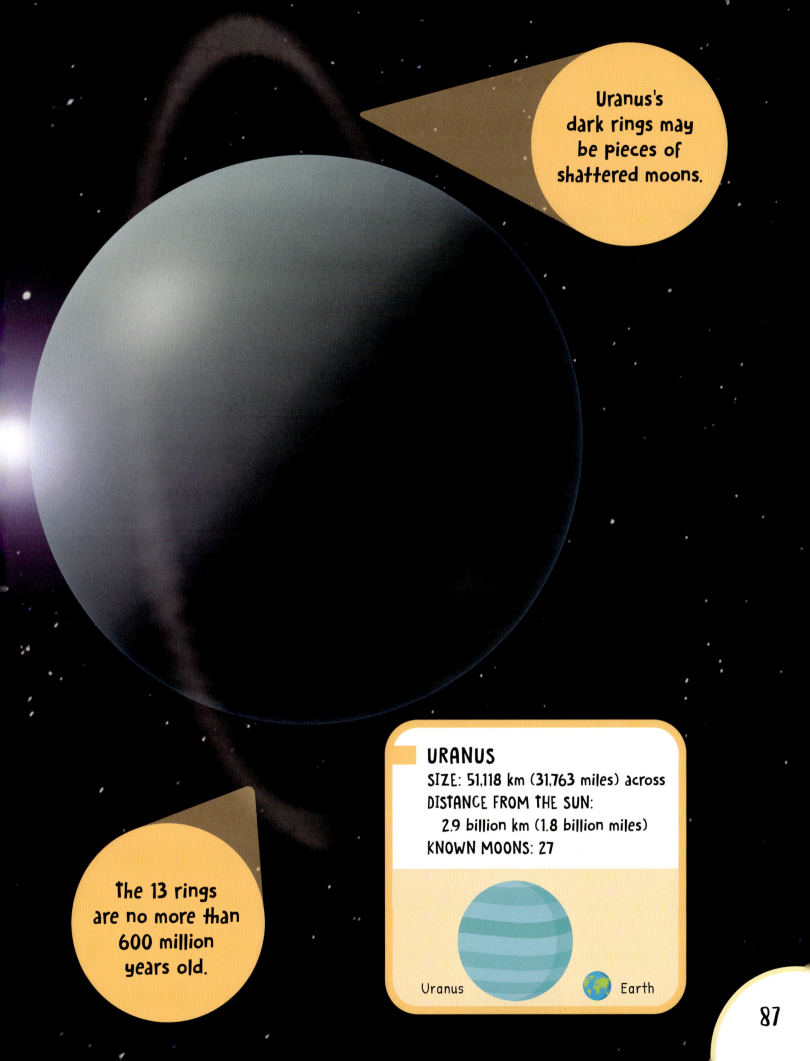

Uranus's dark rings may be pieces of shattered moons.

The 13 rings are no more than 600 million years old.

URANUS

SIZE: 51,118 km (31,763 miles) across
DISTANCE FROM THE SUN:
   2.9 billion km (1.8 billion miles)
KNOWN MOONS: 27

Uranus   Earth

NEPTUNE

As the most distant planet from the Sun, Neptune has the longest orbit. The planet spends 165 years on its journey around the Sun, covering 28.3 billion km (17.6 billion miles).

The Great Dark Spot was a storm seen by the *Voyager 2* space probe in 1989.

Going the Wrong Way!

Neptune's largest moon is named Triton. The Solar System's other large moons orbit their planets in the same direction the planet is rotating. Triton goes the other way! Astronomers think this is because Triton did not form at the same time as Neptune, but was a dwarf planet tugged by Neptune's gravity.

Triton is 2,710 km (1,680 miles) wide.

NEPTUNE

TRITON

PROTEUS

Beyond Neptune

At least four dwarf planets orbit beyond Neptune. From largest to smallest, they are: Pluto, Eris, Haumea, and Makemake. Pluto's orbit is stretched and tilted, so sometimes it travels closer to the Sun than Neptune.

Around 2,376 km (1,476 miles) wide, the dwarf planet Pluto has five moons.

NEPTUNE
SIZE: 49,528 km (30,775 miles) across
DISTANCE FROM THE SUN: 4.5 billion km
   (2.8 billion miles)
KNOWN MOONS: 14

Neptune   Earth

These white streaks are clouds of frozen methane.

THE UNIVERSE

The Universe is more than 93 billion light years across. That means it would take more than 93 billion years for a beam of light to travel across it, past stars, galaxies, and vast areas of emptiness. Yet the Universe is still growing!

UNIVERSE

LOCAL GROUP CLUSTER

Shining Stars

A star is a ball of gas, mostly hydrogen and helium. In a star's tightly squeezed core, tiny particles of hydrogen, called atoms, are constantly crashing together. As they crash, the hydrogen atoms join together to make helium atoms—and release lots of energy.

Energy travels from a star's core to its surface—and then into space. On Earth, we see and feel that energy as light and heat.

Our galaxy is one of around 80 galaxies in our Local Group Cluster.

SOLAR SYSTEM

90

Grouping Galaxies

Stars are grouped into galaxies. These are collections of stars, planets, gas, and dust that are held together by gravity—the force that pulls all objects toward each other. Several galaxies usually group into clusters, which group into superclusters.

Around 160 million light years from Earth, these four galaxies, known as Robert's Quartet, are held together by gravity.

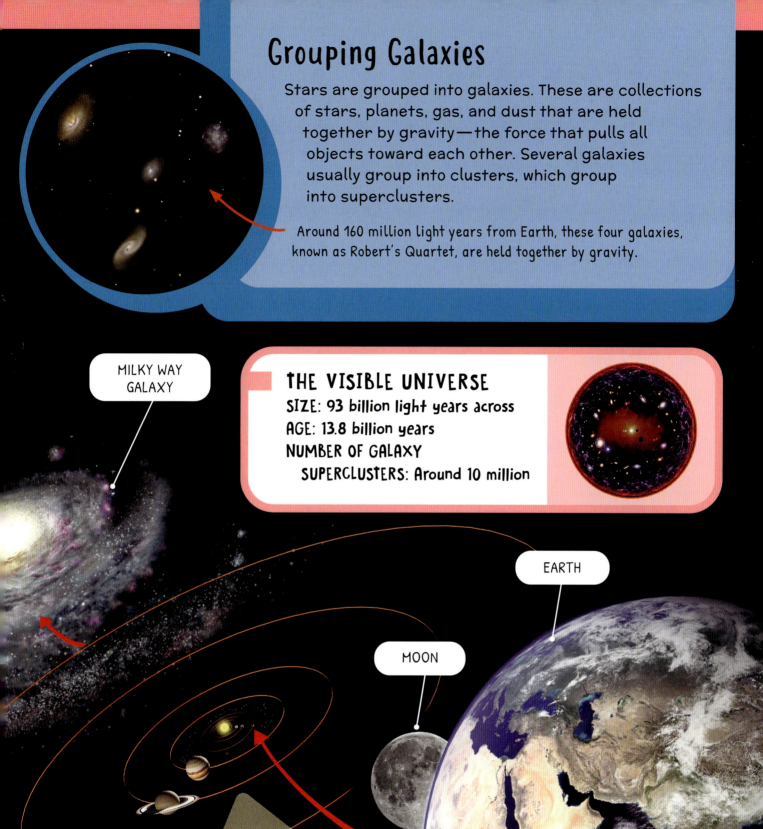

MILKY WAY GALAXY

THE VISIBLE UNIVERSE
SIZE: 93 billion light years across
AGE: 13.8 billion years
NUMBER OF GALAXY
     SUPERCLUSTERS: Around 10 million

EARTH

MOON

Our Solar System is one of billions of solar systems in our galaxy.

TYPES OF STAR

Stars are all different sizes, some much smaller than our Sun and others much more massive! Our Sun is an average-size, average-heat star known as a yellow dwarf.

Never look directly at the Sun, as its brightness will hurt your eyes.

Blue, Yellow, Red ...

The most massive stars are usually the hottest and brightest. The hottest stars give off blue light. Cooler stars shine yellow or—if they are cooler still—red. Smaller stars are named dwarfs, while bigger ones are giants or supergiants.

The biggest supergiants are 2.4 billion km (1.5 billion miles) across.

RED DWARF: TRAPPIST-1

YELLOW DWARF: THE SUN

RED GIANT: ALDEBARAN

BLUE SUPERGIANT: RIGEL

The Sun gives off flares, which are bursts of light.

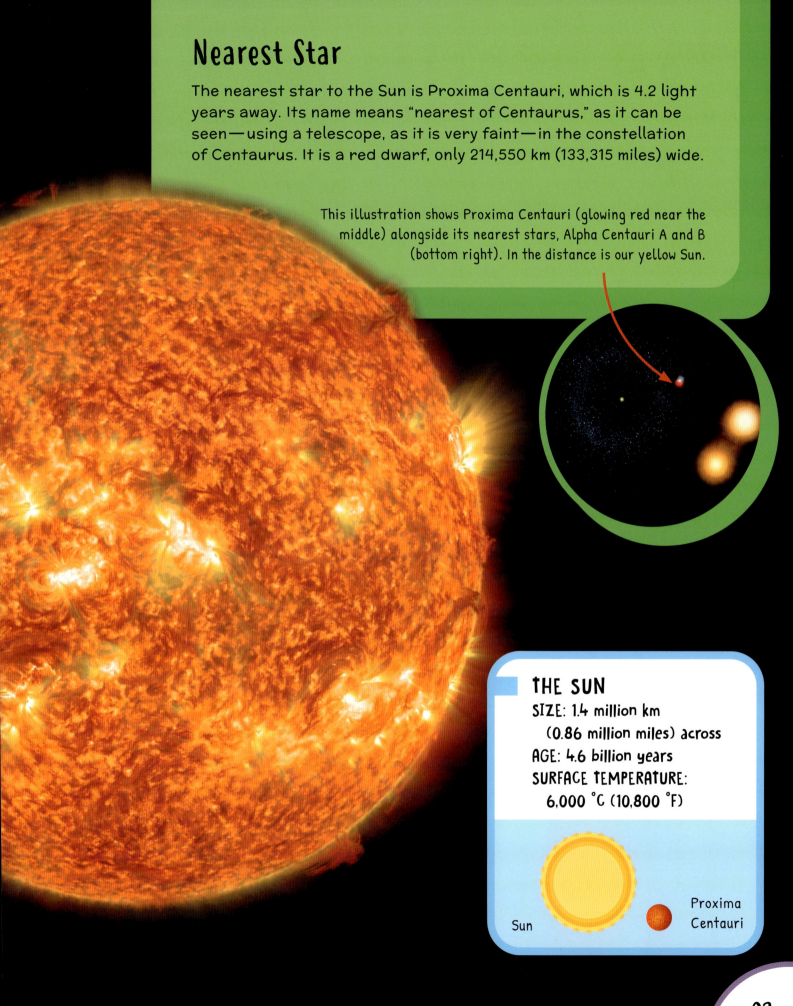

Nearest Star

The nearest star to the Sun is Proxima Centauri, which is 4.2 light years away. Its name means "nearest of Centaurus," as it can be seen—using a telescope, as it is very faint—in the constellation of Centaurus. It is a red dwarf, only 214,550 km (133,315 miles) wide.

This illustration shows Proxima Centauri (glowing red near the middle) alongside its nearest stars, Alpha Centauri A and B (bottom right). In the distance is our yellow Sun.

THE SUN
SIZE: 1.4 million km (0.86 million miles) across
AGE: 4.6 billion years
SURFACE TEMPERATURE: 6,000 °C (10,800 °F)

Sun

Proxima Centauri

STAR BIRTH

Our Sun was born around 4.6 billion years ago, which makes it a middle-aged star! Astronomers think that around 400 million new stars are born every day.

Around 5 light years long, this cloud is a star nursery.

AP COLUMBAE
SIZE: 532,000 km
   (330,000 miles) across
AGE: 40 million years
DISTANCE FROM EARTH:
   27 light years

AP Columbae   Sun

Named the Pillars of Creation, this nursery is 7,000 light years from Earth.

Starting Out

A new star is usually born in a thick cloud of dust and gas. A clump forms in the cloud, its gravity pulling more dust and gas toward it. At last, the ball gets so hot and dense that hydrogen atoms crash together in its core—and a glowing star is born!

A very young star, known as a protostar, is still gathering dust and gas from its cloud.

Star Nurseries

Stars usually form in thick clouds named stellar nurseries (stellar means "star"). However, the closest young star to Earth, AP Columbae, is not in a nursery. It formed when a star exploded, shooting out gas and dust that made new stars!

W51 is one of the biggest star nurseries in the Milky Way.

STAR DEATH

When a star runs out of hydrogen and other fuel, it starts to die. Every star will die eventually. Our Sun will run out of hydrogen in around 5 billion years—long after humans have found somewhere else to live!

the Crab Nebula is a supernova remnant.

How Small Stars Die

When a Sun-sized star runs out of fuel, it swells into a red giant. It throws out gas, making a glowing cloud known as a planetary nebula. Then the star shrinks into a faint white dwarf.

Over billions of years, a white dwarf will stop giving out light, becoming a black dwarf. The Universe is too young for there to be any black dwarfs yet.

SUN-SIZED STAR

RED GIANT

PLANETARY NEBULA

WHITE DWARF

BLACK DWARF

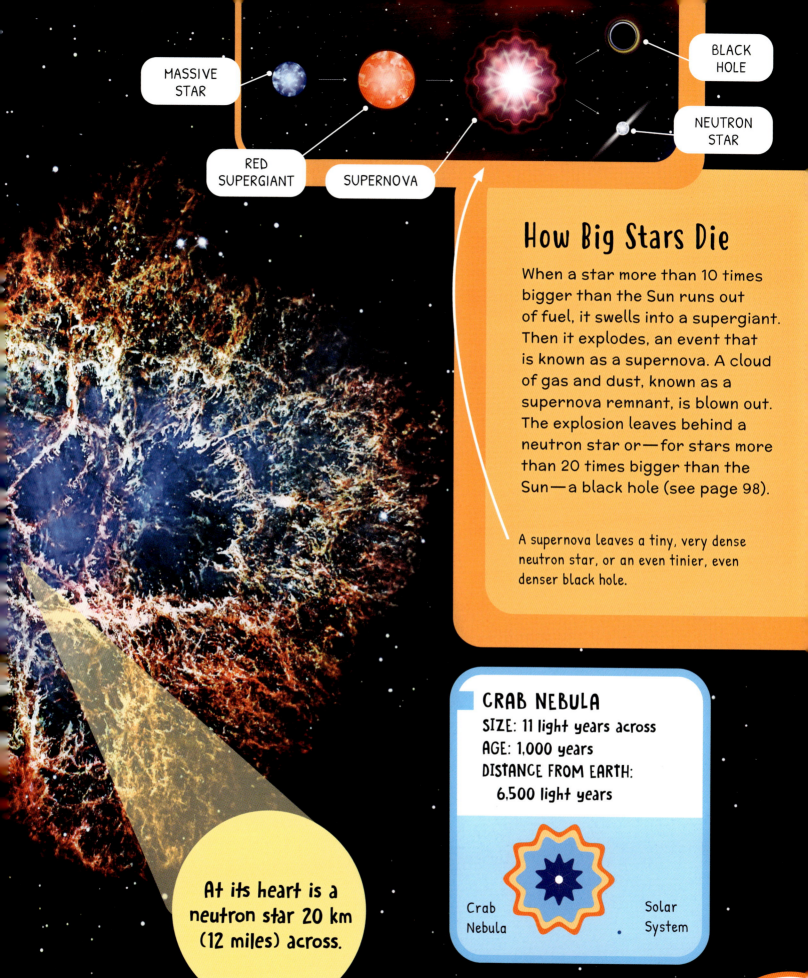

MASSIVE STAR

RED SUPERGIANT

SUPERNOVA

BLACK HOLE

NEUTRON STAR

How Big Stars Die

When a star more than 10 times bigger than the Sun runs out of fuel, it swells into a supergiant. Then it explodes, an event that is known as a supernova. A cloud of gas and dust, known as a supernova remnant, is blown out. The explosion leaves behind a neutron star or—for stars more than 20 times bigger than the Sun—a black hole (see page 98).

A supernova leaves a tiny, very dense neutron star, or an even tinier, even denser black hole.

CRAB NEBULA
SIZE: 11 light years across
AGE: 1,000 years
DISTANCE FROM EARTH: 6,500 light years

Crab Nebula

Solar System

At its heart is a neutron star 20 km (12 miles) across.

BLACK HOLES

A black hole is an area of space with such strong gravity that nothing can escape its pull. It can suck in stars and planets! A black hole can form when a massive star explodes.

This illustration shows the hot dust and gas swirling around a black hole.

SUPERMASSIVE BLACK HOLE M87*
SIZE: 38 billion km (23.6 billion miles) across
MASS: 6 billion Suns
DISTANCE FROM EARTH: 55 million light years

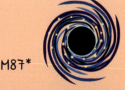
M87*

Solar System

A black hole looks black because it sucks in light.

Great Gravity!

The bigger an object's mass (how heavy it is), the stronger the pull of its gravity. When a black hole is formed by the death of a massive star, the black hole has a mass up to 100 times that of our Sun's. All that mass is packed into an area the size of a city. The strength of a black hole's gravity can deform space.

Within an area called the "event horizon," dust, gas, and stars are sucked into a black hole.

Supermassive Black Holes

There is a supermassive black hole in the middle of most galaxies, including our own. Supermassive black holes have a mass millions of times that of our Sun's. They may form when ordinary black holes grow by sucking in material, or when several stars explode at once.

This photo, taken in 2019, was the first ever taken of a black hole. It shows the supermassive black hole in galaxy M87, surrounded by glowing gas.

99

TYPES OF GALAXY

The smallest galaxies have only a thousand stars, but the biggest have 100 trillion (1 followed by 14 zeros). Smaller galaxies, known as dwarfs, orbit around larger galaxies, known as giants and supergiants.

The Southern Pinwheel Galaxy has a bright central bar.

SOUTHERN PINWHEEL GALAXY
SIZE: 55,000 light years across
NUMBER OF STARS: 40 billion
DISTANCE FROM EARTH: 15 million light years

Southern Pinwheel

Milky Way

This galaxy is a spiral galaxy, with arms of dense gas, dust, and stars.

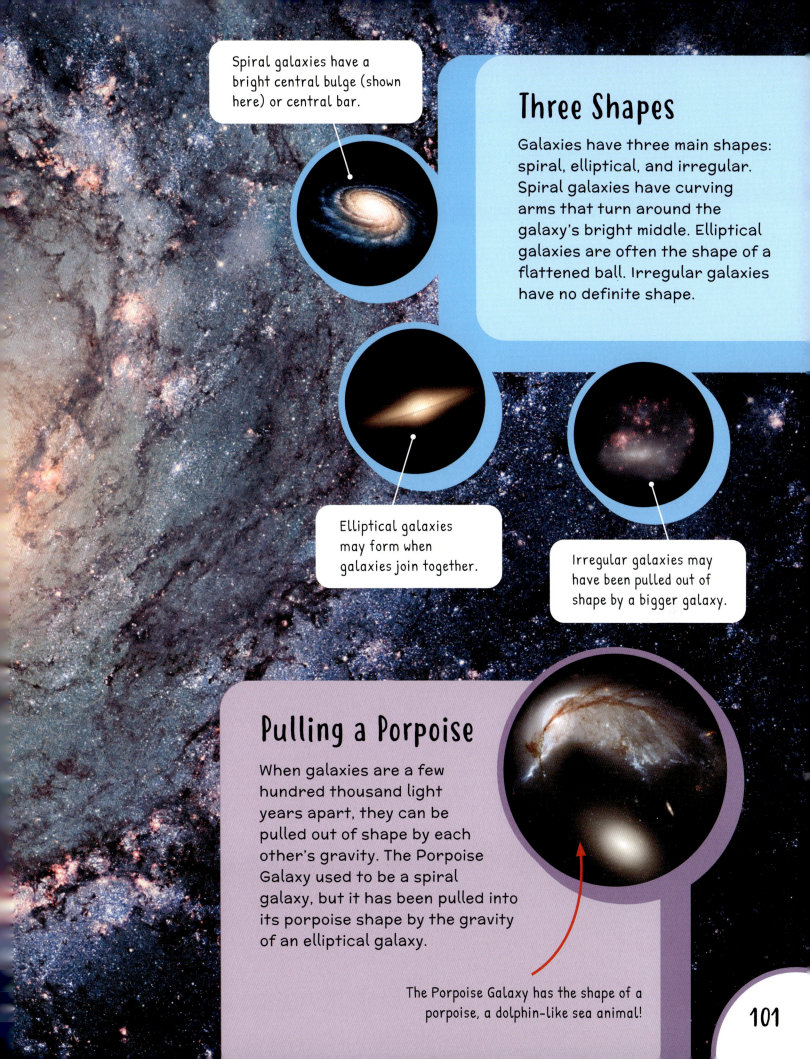

Spiral galaxies have a bright central bulge (shown here) or central bar.

Three Shapes

Galaxies have three main shapes: spiral, elliptical, and irregular. Spiral galaxies have curving arms that turn around the galaxy's bright middle. Elliptical galaxies are often the shape of a flattened ball. Irregular galaxies have no definite shape.

Elliptical galaxies may form when galaxies join together.

Irregular galaxies may have been pulled out of shape by a bigger galaxy.

Pulling a Porpoise

When galaxies are a few hundred thousand light years apart, they can be pulled out of shape by each other's gravity. The Porpoise Galaxy used to be a spiral galaxy, but it has been pulled into its porpoise shape by the gravity of an elliptical galaxy.

The Porpoise Galaxy has the shape of a porpoise, a dolphin-like sea animal!

101

THE MILKY WAY

Our galaxy, named the Milky Way, has around 100 billion stars. That's a lot—if you visited one star per second it would take you 3,100 years to reach them all. The Milky Way is a spiral galaxy with a bar of bright, old stars at its middle.

Getting a Picture

Since our planet is inside the Milky Way's disk, it is difficult to understand the galaxy's shape. It was only in 2019 that telescope photos proved the galaxy has a bar at its middle. Until a spacecraft leaves the galaxy, we will only be able to "see" its whole shape in illustrations.

In the night sky, the edge of the galaxy can be seen as a pale, milky stripe of stars and dust, earning it the name Milky Way.

A supermassive black hole is in our galaxy's central bar.

102

Hangers-On

Around 50 smaller galaxies orbit the Milky Way. They are known as satellite galaxies. The largest is the Large Magellanic Cloud, around 160,000 light years away. It is a dwarf galaxy with a smudged spiral shape due to the pull of our galaxy.

In this photo of the sky over Indonesia, we can see the Large Magellanic Cloud (on the left), and a smaller satellite, the Small Magellanic Cloud (above and to the right).

The galaxy's arms turn at a speed of around 210 km (130 miles) per second.

THE MILKY WAY
SIZE: 105,700 light years across
MASS: 1.5 trillion Suns
AGE: 13.6 billion years

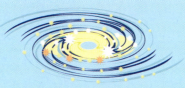

Milky Way

Large Magellanic Cloud

EXOPLANETS

Exoplanets are planets outside our Solar System. Astronomers have discovered over 5,300 exoplanets so far, but they think there are quintillions more in orbit around stars across the Universe.

Nearest Exoplanet

Our nearest exoplanets orbit our nearest star, Proxima Centauri. The two planets are named Proxima b and Proxima c. Proxima b was discovered in 2016, while its sister planet was spotted three years later.

Astronomers think Proxima b has a rocky surface.

Proxima b might look a little like Mars.

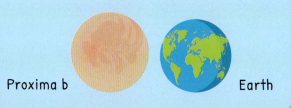

PROXIMA B
SIZE: Possibly around 14,000 km
(8,700 miles) across .
AGE: Around 4.8 billion years
DISTANCE FROM EARTH: 4.2 light years

Proxima b   Earth

Proxima Centauri, and Alpha Centauri A and B, shine in the sky.

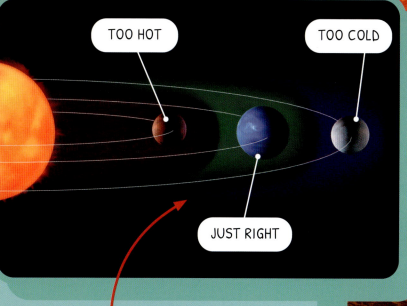

TOO HOT

TOO COLD

JUST RIGHT

Is There Life?

Astronomers study exoplanets to see if they are suitable for living things. For living things to exist, an exoplanet must be the right distance from its star. Proxima b is one of many exoplanets that may be suitable, but no signs of life have been spotted so far.

If a planet is the right temperature, it might have flowing water. All known living things need water.

GALAXY CLUSTERS

Galaxies are often found in clusters. Our galaxy is in the Local Group galaxy cluster, which is in the Virgo Supercluster, part of the even bigger Laniakea Supercluster. This supercluster is part of a galaxy filament known as the Pisces-Cetus Supercluster Complex.

Andromeda is the largest galaxy in the Local Group.

LANIAKEA SUPERCLUSTER

SIZE: 520 million light
 years across
MASS: 100 quadrillion Suns
 (1 followed by 17 zeros)
NUMBER OF GALAXIES: 100,000

The Local Group

Our galaxy cluster contains at least 80 galaxies. The cluster is around 10 million light years across. The three largest galaxies in the cluster are spirals: Andromeda, the Milky Way, and Triangulum.

The Local Group contains the Milky Way and its satellites (lower left), as well as Andromeda and its satellites, shown on the right.

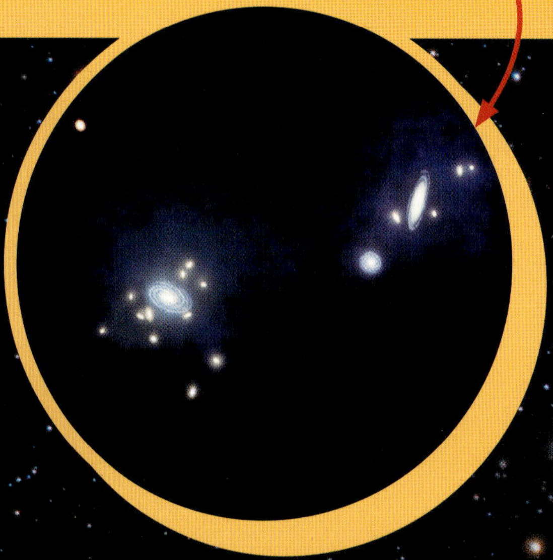

Around 2.5 million light years away, it is 220,000 light years across.

Galaxy Filaments

Galaxy filaments are the largest structures in the Universe. They are made up of galaxy superclusters. Our galaxy filament is 1 billion light years long and 150 million light years wide.

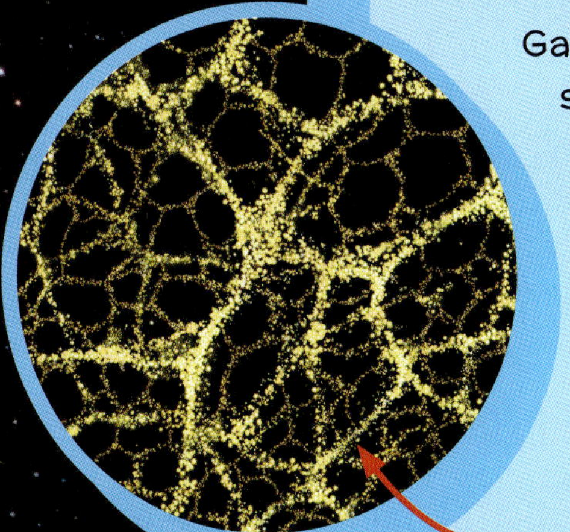

This illustration shows how filaments link together, forming a web. Between the filaments are voids, which contain very few galaxies.

THE BIG BANG

The Universe began 13.8 billion years ago, with what astronomers have named the Big Bang. In that first moment, the Universe started to grow from a tiny, very hot point. After 100 million years, the first stars were born.

200 MILLION YEARS

100 MILLION YEARS

300,000 YEARS

Atoms start to form. They are the building blocks for stars and people.

THE BIG BANG
WHEN: 13.8 billion years ago
SIZE OF UNIVERSE AFTER 1 SECOND:
    Around 18 light years across
TEMPERATURE OF UNIVERSE AFTER 1 SECOND:
    1 quadrillion °C (1.8 quadrillion °F)

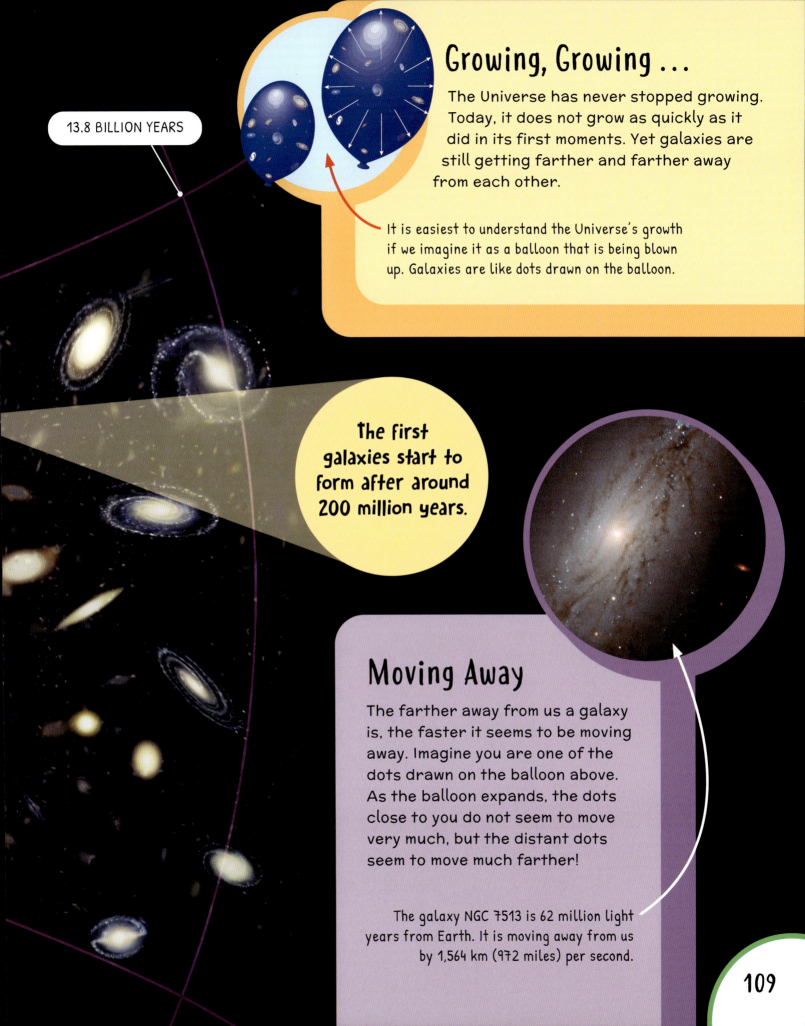

Growing, Growing ...

The Universe has never stopped growing. Today, it does not grow as quickly as it did in its first moments. Yet galaxies are still getting farther and farther away from each other.

It is easiest to understand the Universe's growth if we imagine it as a balloon that is being blown up. Galaxies are like dots drawn on the balloon.

the first galaxies start to form after around 200 million years.

Moving Away

The farther away from us a galaxy is, the faster it seems to be moving away. Imagine you are one of the dots drawn on the balloon above. As the balloon expands, the dots close to you do not seem to move very much, but the distant dots seem to move much farther!

The galaxy NGC 7513 is 62 million light years from Earth. It is moving away from us by 1,564 km (972 miles) per second.

WATCHING THE SKY

We can watch the night sky with our bare eyes or—to see more distant objects—with binoculars or a telescope. The most powerful telescopes on Earth have the power of 4 million human eyes!

How Telescopes Work

We can see stars and galaxies because they give off light, which enters our eyes. Telescopes use mirrors to gather more light than human eyes can collect. Telescopes also use curved pieces of glass, known as lenses, to magnify images (make them bigger), so that distant objects become clearer.

In a reflecting telescope, the curving primary mirror collects lots of light.

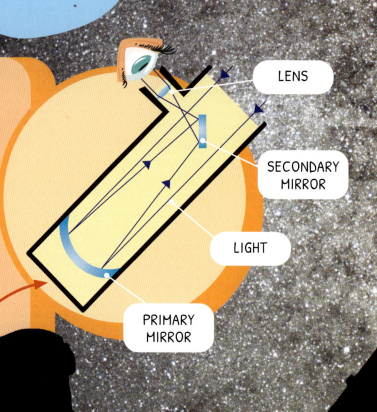

LENS

SECONDARY MIRROR

LIGHT

PRIMARY MIRROR

With our bare eyes, we can see stars up to 4,000 light years away.

Biggest Telescope

The biggest single-mirrored telescope on Earth is the Gran Telescopio Canarias, in Spain. It is powerful enough to study black holes and planets orbiting distant stars.

Like other large telescopes, the Gran Telescopio Canarias is on a mountaintop, where its view is not spoiled by bad weather, pollution, or light from cities.

A store-bought telescope can reveal galaxies millions of light years away.

GRAN TELESCOPIO CANARIAS

SIZE OF PRIMARY MIRROR: 10.4 m (34.1 ft) across

IN ACTION: Since 2007

EQUIPMENT: Mirrors for gathering light, as well as instruments for collecting infrared energy

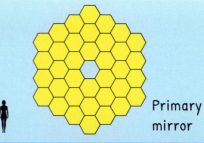

Primary mirror

CONSTELLATIONS

Constellations are groups of stars that form a pattern in the night sky. The stars in a constellation are often many light years apart, but they look close together when seen from Earth!

The bright star Sirius is in the Canis Major ("Greater Dog") constellation.

Northern Constellations

Astronomers agree on 88 constellations. More than half of them can be seen from north of the equator during some or all of the year. The ancient Greeks named 48 of these constellations after people and animals from their myths.

This nineteenth-century star map shows the constellation Perseus, named after a Greek hero who cut the head off a monster.

The Orion constellation can be spotted by the three stars in the hunter's belt.

Southern Constellations

Many of the southern constellations were given their official names after the sixteenth century. Some are named after scientific instruments, such as a microscope (Microscopium) or telescope (Telescopium).

Microscopium (left) and Telescopium (right) are on either side of Sagittarius, who was a mythological centaur with the upper body of a human and the legs of a horse.

ORION CONSTELLATION
DISTANCE OF NEAREST STAR
   FROM EARTH: 245 light years
CAN BE SEEN: Across the world
NAMED AFTER: A hunter in Greek
   mythology who had a dog named Sirius

POLE STARS

As Earth turns around its axis, the stars seem to rotate around us—even though it is us moving, not them! Only the stars above the north and south poles seem to stay still. Knowing how to find the pole stars is useful for finding our way at night.

the other stars seem to rotate around the North Star.

North Pole Star

The North Star is the brightest star in the constellation of Ursa Minor ("Little Bear"). Although it looks like a single star, it is actually three stars orbiting each other, around 433 light years away.

To find the North Star and know which direction is north, follow a line from the "big dipper" (or "plough") shape in the nearby constellation of Ursa Major ("Great Bear").

URSA MINOR

NORTH STAR

BIG DIPPER

South Pole Star

The South Star is a faint star in the constellation of Octans. It is a single, giant star around 294 light years from Earth.

The South Star is just outside the triangle of Octans, which is named after a measuring instrument: the octant.

OCTANS

SOUTH STAR

If many photos are taken during one night, they can be combined to show star trails.

URSA MAJOR CONSTELLATION
DISTANCE OF NEAREST STAR FROM
EARTH: 8 light years
CAN BE SEEN: From most of the
northern hemisphere
NAMED AFTER: A mother bear
in Greek mythology

ECLIPSES

An eclipse is when a planet, moon, or star is hidden for a few moments, either because another object passes in front of it, or because it moves into the shadow of another object. We can see eclipses of the Sun and Moon every few years.

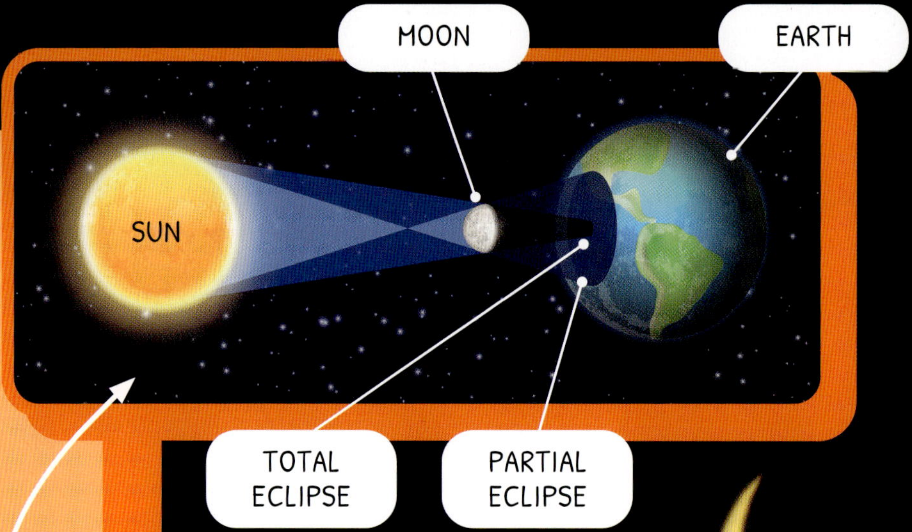

MOON

EARTH

SUN

TOTAL ECLIPSE

PARTIAL ECLIPSE

Eclipses of the Sun

An eclipse of the Sun happens when the Moon passes between Earth and the Sun, hiding the Sun. It can happen only when the Sun, Moon, and Earth are in a perfectly straight line.

A total eclipse of the Sun can be seen around once every 18 months from somewhere on Earth.

This step-by-step picture shows the Moon crossing the Sun.

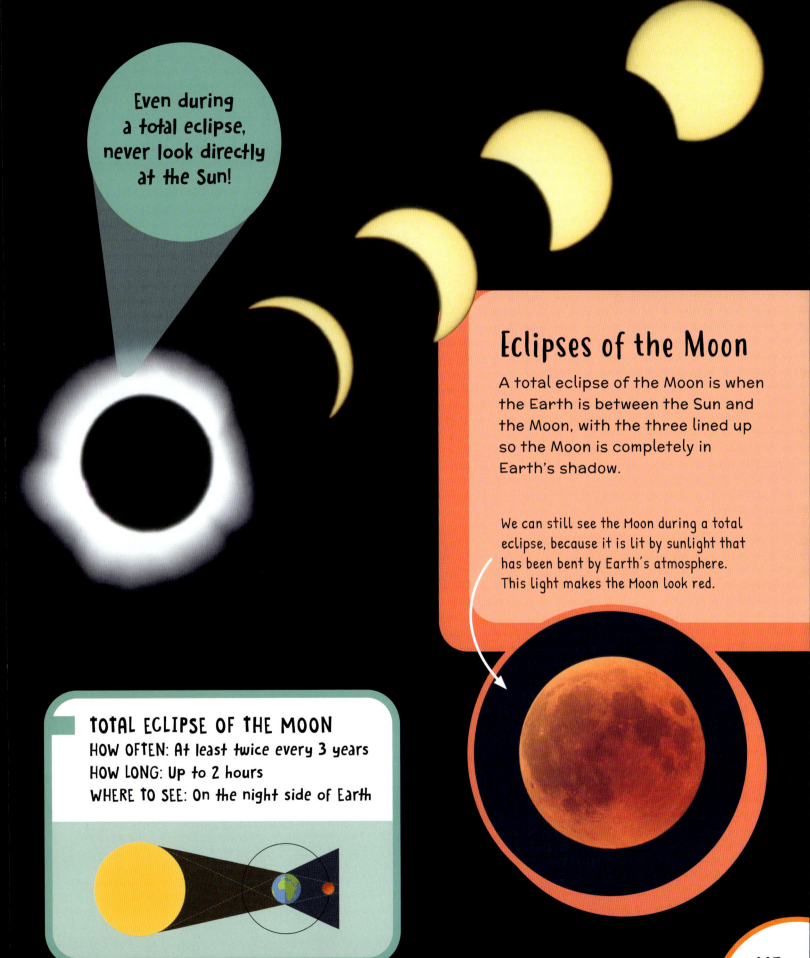

Even during a total eclipse, never look directly at the Sun!

Eclipses of the Moon

A total eclipse of the Moon is when the Earth is between the Sun and the Moon, with the three lined up so the Moon is completely in Earth's shadow.

We can still see the Moon during a total eclipse, because it is lit by sunlight that has been bent by Earth's atmosphere. This light makes the Moon look red.

TOTAL ECLIPSE OF THE MOON
HOW OFTEN: At least twice every 3 years
HOW LONG: Up to 2 hours
WHERE TO SEE: On the night side of Earth

COMETS

A comet is an icy ball of dust and rock that orbits the Sun. A comet's orbit is so stretched and long that it travels both close to and very far from the Sun. When a comet nears the Sun, it heats up—and may be seen as a bright streak in the sky.

Growing Tails

As a comet moves inside Mars's orbit around the Sun, it gets hot enough to release gas, which can be seen as a streaming, glowing tail. As a comet nears the Sun, a second tail grows, made of dust.

A comet's gas tail is always blown away from the Sun.

COMET'S ORBIT

GAS TAIL

DUST TAIL

EARTH'S ORBIT

COMET HALLEY
HOW OFTEN: Last seen in 1986,
  it will reappear in 2061
HOW LONG: A few days
WHERE TO SEE: Away from city lights

The comet's gas tail stretched for millions of miles.

Comet Neowise was seen from Earth in 2020 and will reappear in 6,800 years.

Long and Short

Comet Encke has the shortest orbit around the Sun: 3.3 years. The comet with the longest known orbit is Comet West, which journeys for at least 254,000 years. However, there may be comets with much longer orbits that we have not spotted yet!

Comet Halley has an orbit of 75–76 years. Shortly after it was seen in 1066, the comet was stitched into the famous Bayeux Tapestry.

ISTI MIRANT STELLA

MISSIONS TO SPACE

Astronomers say that space begins 100 km (62 miles) above Earth's surface. A rocket was the first human-made object to enter space, in 1949. It was another 12 years before a human reached space.

Brave Astronauts

In 1961, the first human in space was the Soviet Union's Yuri Gagarin. Since then, more than 500 people have visited space. Most of them have been highly trained astronauts, but since 2001, a few have been space tourists, who paid for their trip.

Yuri Gagarin is strapped into his Vostok 3KA space capsule, before blasting off to make one orbit around Earth.

American astronaut Mae Jemison orbited Earth 127 times.

Where Have Humans Been?

Humans have orbited Earth and the Moon many times, but the Moon is the only place, apart from Earth, where humans have set foot. However, uncrewed spacecraft have landed on—or deliberately crashed into—Mercury, Venus, Mars, Jupiter, Saturn, and its moon Titan, and a few asteroids and comets.

Saturn has no solid surface to land on, but the *Cassini* spacecraft flew into the planet's atmosphere, where it managed to send home information before it was destroyed.

VOSTOK 3KA
SIZE: 4.6 m (15 ft) long and 2.4 m (7.9 ft) wide
IN ACTION: 1961–63
EQUIPMENT: Braking engine and escape system

ROCKETS

All spacecraft are lifted into space by a rocket. Once a rocket has done its work, it separates from its spacecraft —and either stays in space or falls to Earth, where it lands harmlessly in the ocean.

A Russian Soyuz-2 rocket lifts off from Kazakhstan.

Up, Up, and Away

To beat the pull of Earth's gravity, a rocket must reach a speed of 40,000 km/h (25,000 miles per hour). To do this, a rocket needs lots of fuel, which is burned in its engines to release a blast of gas. By blasting the gas downward, the rocket shoots upward—like how kicking water backward makes you swim forward!

A rocket has nozzles through which it blasts hot gas.

the Soyuz MS-19 spacecraft carries crew to the International Space Station.

In Stages

Rockets have between two and five parts—called stages—each with its own engines and fuel. When a rocket takes off, only its first stage fires its engine. When that stage has burned its fuel, it is dropped. The next stage takes over, then is dropped, and so on. The remaining rocket weighs less and less, so it can fly faster.

This illustration shows the inside (left) and outside (right) of the Saturn V rocket, which lifted all the human missions to the Moon.

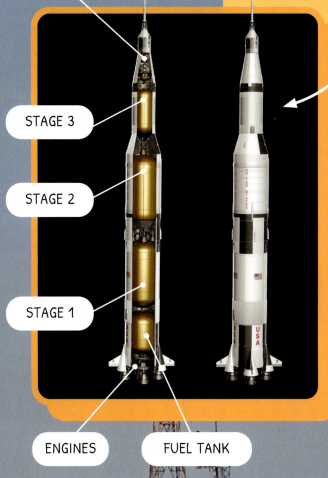

SPACECRAFT

STAGE 3

STAGE 2

STAGE 1

ENGINES

FUEL TANK

SOYUZ-2
SIZE: 46.3 m (152 ft) tall and 2.95 m (9.7 ft) wide
IN ACTION: From 2004
EQUIPMENT: two stages for low orbits or three stages for higher orbits

SPACE CAPSULES

Most spacecraft that have carried humans have been space capsules. While in space, a space capsule is steered using its engines, which blast in different directions. But a space capsule has no wings, so, once it has completed its mission, it falls to Earth!

Neil Armstrong took this photo of Buzz Aldrin on the Moon.

Falling Down

A space capsule's fall through Earth's atmosphere is slowed by a parachute or backward-blasting engines. It lands in the ocean or desert. Although the crew is cushioned, most space capsules are designed to be used only once, as they are damaged by the impact.

Launched in 2020, *Crew Dragon 2* is a space capsule that carries crew to the International Space Station.

Armstrong and the lunar module are reflected in Aldrin's helmet.

APOLLO COMMAND MODULE

SIZE: 3.2 m (10.6 ft) tall and 3.9 m (12.8 ft) wide

IN ACTION: 1966–75

EQUIPMENT: Seats, food, water, engines, parachutes, and around 700 controls and displays

Walking on the Moon

The first humans on the Moon were US astronauts Neil Armstrong and Edwin "Buzz" Aldrin, in 1969. Their Apollo space capsule had three parts: the command module, which was the cabin and the only part that returned to Earth; the service module, which held the engine; and the lunar module.

LUNAR MODULE

The lunar module flew to the Moon's surface, while the command and service modules, along with astronaut Michael Collins, remained in orbit around the Moon.

COMMAND MODULE

SERVICE MODULE

SPACEPLANES

Unlike space capsules, spaceplanes have wings, so they can fly down to Earth, then land like an ordinary plane. This means they can be re-used. Despite this benefit, there have not been many spaceplanes—so far!

Space Shuttle

The most successful spaceplanes were the United States' five Space Shuttles, which flew 135 missions before they were retired in 2011. They carried crew to the International Space Station and positioned satellites in orbit around Earth.

To lift off, a Space Shuttle fired its engines, which used fuel from a large orange fuel tank, and got extra power from two white booster rockets. The tank and boosters were dropped after launch.

A Space Shuttle weighed 75,000 kg (165,000 lb) when empty.

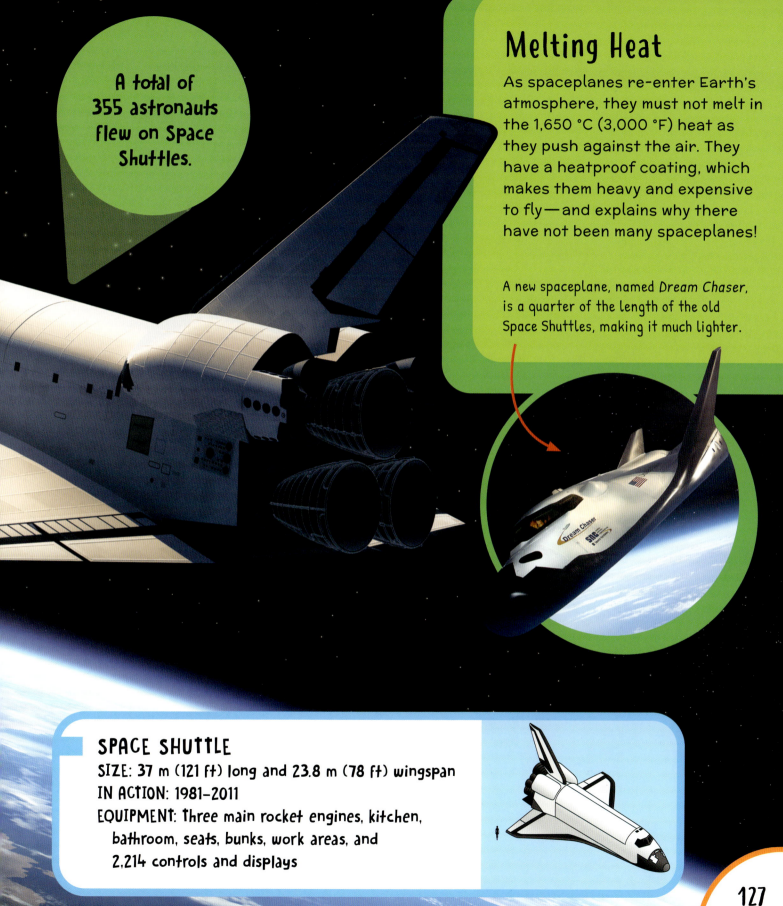

A total of 355 astronauts flew on Space Shuttles.

Melting Heat

As spaceplanes re-enter Earth's atmosphere, they must not melt in the 1,650 °C (3,000 °F) heat as they push against the air. They have a heatproof coating, which makes them heavy and expensive to fly—and explains why there have not been many spaceplanes!

A new spaceplane, named *Dream Chaser*, is a quarter of the length of the old Space Shuttles, making it much lighter.

SPACE SHUTTLE
SIZE: 37 m (121 ft) long and 23.8 m (78 ft) wingspan
IN ACTION: 1981–2011
EQUIPMENT: three main rocket engines, kitchen, bathroom, seats, bunks, work areas, and 2,214 controls and displays

SATELLITES

A human-made satellite is a machine that is placed in orbit around Earth—or another planet or moon. The first satellite, the Soviet Union's *Sputnik 1*, went into orbit in 1957. Today, there are at least 5,000 satellites orbiting our planet.

Landsat 9 takes photos of Earth's forests and cities to see how they change.

What Do They Do?

Some satellites orbiting Earth are watching the weather, or taking photos of sea ice or wildfires. Others are communications satellites, which bounce TV, phone, and internet signals around the world. Many satellites are used for navigation (finding the way).

If a car "satnav" (satellite navigation device) receives signals from three navigation satellites, it knows how far away each satellite is, and can calculate where it is.

Why Don't They Fall?

Satellites are pulled toward Earth by its gravity, but at the same time they are speeding along at more than 10,000 km/h (6,000 miles per hour). This means that their fall is curved so they circle Earth rather than dropping onto it.

A satellite gains its speed from the rocket that lifted it into space. Without anything to slow the satellite down, it carries on moving at the same speed—which makes it orbit.

Satellite speeds in this direction.

Gravity pulls toward Earth.

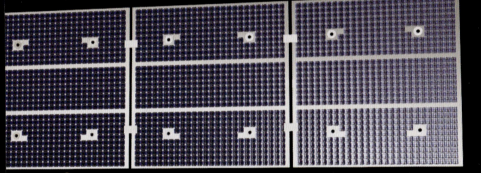

A solar panel turns sunlight into electricity to power the cameras.

LANDSAT 9
SIZE: **3 m (9.8 ft) long and 4.6 m (15 ft) wide**
IN ACTION: Since 2021
EQUIPMENT: Cameras that take photos and also reveal the temperatures of Earth's surface

129

INTERNATIONAL SPACE STATION

The International Space Station (ISS) is a huge satellite where astronauts live and work for months at a time. It orbits 400 km (250 miles) above Earth. The space station was put together in orbit, section by section, by astronauts.

Falling and Floating

Astronauts float around inside the ISS. This is because the ISS experiences microgravity, where people and objects appear to be weightless. As Earth's gravity pulls on the ISS and its astronauts, both the people and the space station fall toward Earth (but it is a curving, never-ending fall; see page 129). As everything falls together, people appear to float!

Microgravity does not mean there is no gravity, just that gravity appears to have little effect!

INTERNATIONAL SPACE STATION

SIZE: 109 m (358 ft) long and
 73 m (239 ft) wide
IN ACTION: From 1998
EQUIPMENT: Areas for working, sleeping,
 exercising, cooking, and washing; water and
 oxygen supplies; solar panels and batteries

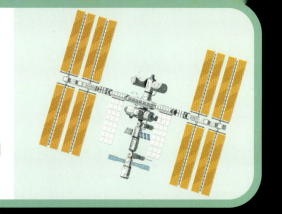

The 34-m-
(112-ft)-long
solar panels can
turn to face
the Sun.

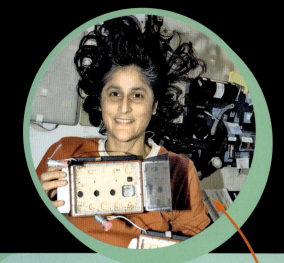

Working Hard

Astronauts from 19 countries have worked onboard the ISS. They observe Earth and space. They also work in four science laboratories, run by Europe, Japan, Russia, and the United States.

Astronaut Sunita Williams holds a home containing Nefertiti the spider during an experiment to see how spiders behave in space. Nefertiti returned safely to Earth.

Spacecraft can
dock here to
unload astronauts
and supplies.

131

FUTURE MISSIONS

One day, humans could travel outside the Solar System. But using the rockets we have now, it would take us a thousand years to reach the nearest star! We would need food, water, and oxygen to breathe during the journey. For now, we will stay closer to home ...

The Launch Abort System pulls the capsule away from its rocket in an emergency.

The new Orion space capsule could carry humans to Mars.

Back to the Moon

Only 12 humans, all of them men, have walked on the Moon—and no one has set foot there since 1972. There are plans for humans, including at least one woman, to return to the Moon within the next 10 years.

The United States plans to build a base on the Moon, where astronauts will be able to live for months at a time.

ORION

SIZE: 6 m (19.7 ft) long and 5 m (16 ft) wide
IN ACTION: Since 2022
EQUIPMENT: Seats, bunks, bathroom, engines, four computers, and 67 switches

Journey to the Red Planet

China, Europe, Russia, and the United States hope to send humans to Mars within the next 20 to 50 years. As Earth and Mars travel around the Sun, the shortest distance between them is 55 million km (34 million miles). The journey would take at least seven months.

If astronauts built a base on Mars, they would need to take machines and materials to make water, oxygen, and food.

ANIMALS

From ants to whales, animals live almost everywhere on Earth. All animals are in one of six groups. There are mammals, reptiles, birds, fish, amphibians, and invertebrates.

Many Habitats

An animal's habitat is where it lives, from the oceans, to caves or forests. Each animal's body is suited to its habitat, whether it is hot or cold, dark or light, in water or on land.

Camels store fat in their humps, so they can last without food in the desert.

Different Lives

Some animals give birth to live babies, while others lay eggs. Baby meerkats and sharks look like their parents, but a baby caterpillar must change shape to become a butterfly.

This boxer crab is carrying its red eggs on its front.

Finding Food

Every animal is perfectly shaped for finding its food. Lions have sharp teeth for gripping zebras. Octopuses have long arms for catching fish.

A toucan grabs fruit with its large beak.

The Jezebel butterfly is an invertebrate, with no bones at all.

It is sucking flower nectar.

MAMMALS

Mammals have skeletons made of bone. Most mammals have four legs, which they use to walk on land. Yet some mammals have bodies suited to flying, swimming, or jumping. A few, such as humans, can walk on two legs!

Hippopotamuses wallow in water to keep cool and damp.

Like all mammals, hippos can breathe air through their nostrils.

Caring for Young

Nearly all mammals give birth to live babies. Mothers feed their babies on milk they make inside their own body. Mammals usually look after their young until they are big enough to take care of themselves.

This meerkat mother is feeding her pups on milk.

HIPPOPOTAMUS
HOW BIG: 3.3 to 5.2 m (11 to 17 ft) long
HOME: Around lakes and rivers in Africa
FOOD: Grass

Being Hairy

All mammals grow hair. Many mammals have thick hair called fur. Fur has short, warm hairs and longer, waterproof hairs. Whales and other mammals that live in water have very little hair, because it would get soggy!

A polar bear's thick fur helps keep it warm in the Arctic.

CATS

Lions, tigers, cheetahs, leopards, jaguars, and wildcats are in the cat family. Thousands of years ago, the first pet cats were captured wildcats. A cat's fur helps with camouflage, as the shade and pattern make the cat harder to spot.

A male lion's mane protects its neck during fights.

Hunters

Cats are meat-eaters. They have 30 sharp teeth for biting into flesh. When their claws are not needed for grasping prey, they are pulled back into the fur around the toes.

This lucky bird is escaping from a Siberian tiger.

Fast Runners

With a muscly body and strong legs, cats are fast runners, although they soon get tired. Cats usually creep up on their prey, then suddenly run forward and pounce.

The cheetah is the world's fastest runner, reaching up to 112 km/h (70 miles per hour).

LION

HOW BIG: 1.6 to 2 m (5.2 to 6.6 ft) long
HOME: Grassland, mainly in Africa
FOOD: Zebras, wildebeest, and goats

Sensitive whiskers help feel the way when it is dark.

DOGS

Dogs usually live in families or bigger groups. They have sharp teeth, long legs, and bushy tails. Dogs live everywhere except Antarctica. Wolves, foxes, coyotes, dingoes, wild dogs, and pet dogs are all in the dog family.

Gray wolves live in groups called packs.

Play Fighting

Young dogs often have pretend fights. This is a way to try out and perfect their skills. Play fighting helps them make friends, but also shows which dogs are tougher. The toughest dogs will become leaders.

These red fox cubs are careful not to hurt each other.

GRAY WOLF
HOW BIG: 1.2 to 1.8 m
(4 to 6 ft) long
HOME: Remote parts of Asia, Europe, and North America
FOOD: Deer, bison, beavers, and mice

Senses

Dogs have an excellent sense of smell for finding each other and tracking down prey. Most dogs have upright ears to capture even the quietest sounds.

The African wild dog can turn its huge ears to hear sounds better.

Wolves howl to keep in touch with each other.

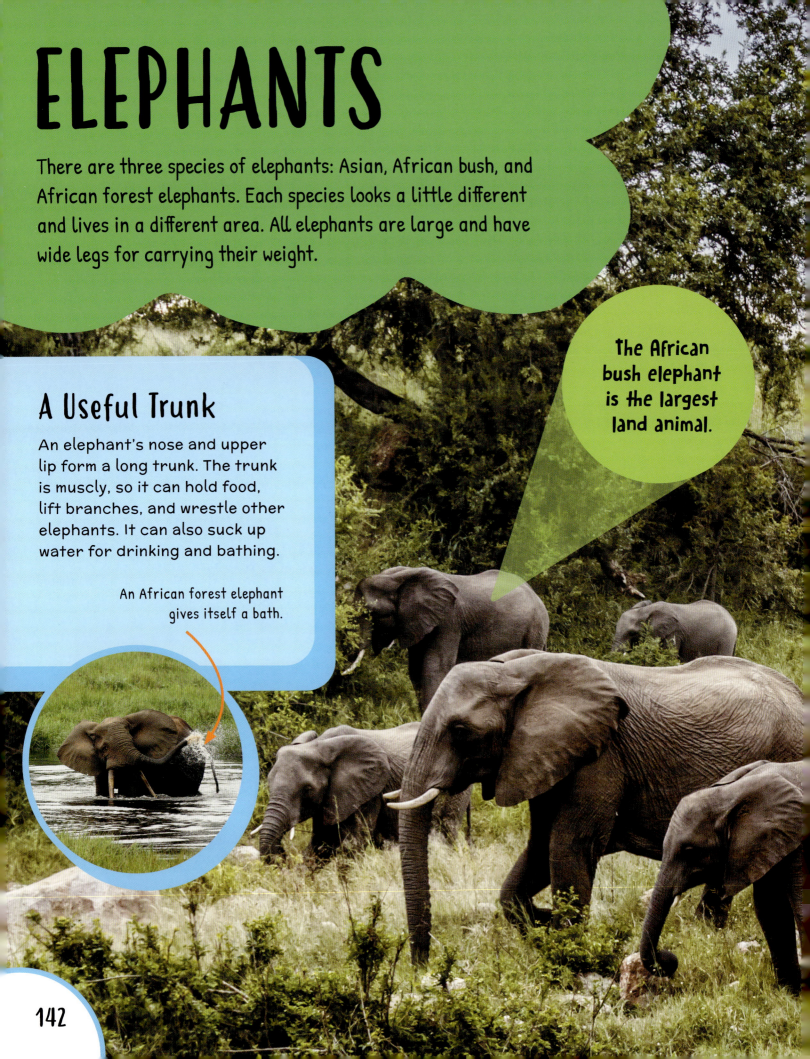

ELEPHANTS

There are three species of elephants: Asian, African bush, and African forest elephants. Each species looks a little different and lives in a different area. All elephants are large and have wide legs for carrying their weight.

The African bush elephant is the largest land animal.

A Useful Trunk

An elephant's nose and upper lip form a long trunk. The trunk is muscly, so it can hold food, lift branches, and wrestle other elephants. It can also suck up water for drinking and bathing.

An African forest elephant gives itself a bath.

In Danger

Elephants are in danger of extinction. They are at risk because some people kill them to sell their tusks, which are made of beautiful ivory. Many countries are working to keep their elephants safe.

An Asian elephant uses its tusks for fighting, lifting, and digging.

Baby elephants often hold their mother's tail.

AFRICAN BUSH ELEPHANT
HOW BIG: 5 to 7 m (16 to 24 ft) long
HOME: Grassland, woodland, and
       wetland in Africa
FOOD: Grasses, leaves, and tree bark

MARSUPIALS

Koalas, kangaroos, wallabies, wombats, and possums are marsupials. Marsupials live in Australia and nearby islands, or in the Americas. Most marsupial mothers have a pouch for carrying around their babies.

The Pouch

Other mammals do not give birth until their baby has grown quite big and strong. But marsupial babies are born much earlier, when they are just the size of a jellybean —or even smaller. After birth, a baby marsupial usually crawls inside its mother's pouch, where it is warm and safe.

A young kangaroo, called a joey, does not leave the pouch until it is eight months old.

Gliders

Gliding possums have flaps of skin that stretch between their front and back legs. They launch themselves from a tree branch and spread their legs, then float down to a lower branch.

The sugar glider can glide for up to 50 m (164 ft).

KOALA

HOW BIG: 60 to 85 cm (24 to 33 in) long
HOME: Woodland and forest in Australia
FOOD: Leaves, usually from eucalyptus trees

Big, round ears give a koala good hearing.

A koala's curved, sharp claws help it grip onto trees.

145

MONKEYS AND APES

Monkeys and apes are primates. Millions of years ago, all primates lived in trees and had tails. Today, most primates live in trees, but some live on the ground. Most monkeys still have a tail, but apes do not.

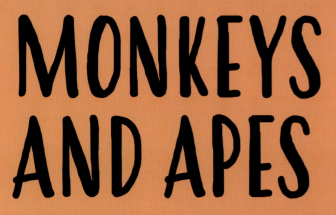

SUMATRAN ORANGUTAN

HOW BIG: 90 to 150 cm (3 to 5 ft) long

HOME: Rain forest in Sumatra, in Asia

FOOD: Fruit, insects, and tree bark

Close Cousins

Humans are actually apes! Our closest relatives are chimpanzees and bonobos. Like us, they live in groups and make sounds to each other. They spend lots of time on the ground. They are clever, using sticks and stones as simple tools.

This chimpanzee has collected insects to eat, by using a stick.

These large apes can grip branches with their toes.

A baby orangutan is carried until it is five years old.

An Extra Hand

Many Central and South American monkeys have a tail that can curl around branches, like an extra hand. These are called prehensile tails. They are useful for swinging from branch to branch.

A spider monkey dangles from its prehensile tail.

WHALES AND DOLPHINS

Most whales and dolphins live in the sea, but a few dolphins live in rivers. These swimming mammals have a pair of flippers and a flat tail. Dolphins are part of the whale family. They are usually smaller and have cone-shaped teeth.

the biggest dolphin, an orca, can swim at 56 km/h (35 miles per hour).

It comes to the surface to breathe air through its blowhole.

ORCA
HOW BIG: 5 to 8 m (16 to 26 ft) long
HOME: All oceans
FOOD: Fish, squid, seals, birds, and turtles

Living in a Pod

Whales and dolphins usually live in groups, called pods. They "talk" to each other by making noises. Dolphins make clicks and whistles. Whales grunt and groan. Some whales use these sounds in long "songs" to each other.

Baby bottlenose dolphins swim close to their mothers.

Feeding

All dolphins and some whales have teeth, for snapping up fish or squid. Other whales have bristles in their mouth. They feed by filling their mouth with seawater. Tiny creatures in the water are trapped inside the whale's mouth by the bristles.

A humpback whale uses its bristles to catch small fish and krill.

REPTILES

Snakes, lizards, turtles, and crocodiles are reptiles. Many reptiles have four legs, but all snakes and some lizards have become legless. Most reptiles lay eggs on land.

Like all reptiles, the tuatara sheds its skin when it is outgrown.

Cold-Blooded

Most reptiles are cold-blooded, which means their bodies cannot make heat to keep them warm. Many reptiles bask in the sun to warm up. If they get too hot, they move into the shade, or go for a swim.

This gharial is basking in the sun. Gharials are related to crocodiles.

TUATARA
HOW BIG: 45 to 80 cm (18 to 31 in) long
HOME: Forests on small islands in New Zealand
FOOD: Worms, insects, lizards, frogs, and birds

Scales

A reptile's skin is protected by hard plates called scales. Turtles and crocodiles have larger, bonier plates than other reptiles. Scales contain keratin, which is also in human nails.

This reptile's small scales are lined up in rings.

A tuatara's crest is made of spiky scales.

SNAKES

Most snakes move forward by wriggling their bodies from side to side. Many snakes live on the ground, but some swim in water or crawl in trees. Their jaws open wide so they can swallow large prey without chewing.

The eyelash viper grips flowers and branches with its tail.

Venom

There are 3,600 species of snakes, but only around 600 make venom. Venom is a poison injected into prey using long, hollow teeth called fangs. Venom kills prey or stops it moving.

A spitting cobra can inject or spray venom from its fangs.

EYELASH VIPER
HOW BIG: 55 to 82 cm
(22 to 32 in) long
HOME: Rain forests in
the Americas
FOOD: Mice, frogs, lizards,
and birds

Scales above
its eyes look
like eyelashes.

Constriction

Some snakes kill their prey by
constriction. First, the snake
bites its prey, holding tight
while coiling around it. Then
the snake squeezes until the
animal's blood cannot flow and
its heart stops beating.

This boa constrictor has
wrapped itself around its prey.

153

LIZARDS

Lizards are many different sizes and shapes. The littlest are geckos just 2 cm (0.8 in) long, while the largest is the fierce Komodo dragon. Most lizards have four legs, a tail, and a long tongue.

Special Signals

Lizards often signal to each other. Male lizards signal to get a female's attention. Some signal to scare other lizards away. Signals can include mouth opening, tail wagging, push-ups, or showing off bright body parts.

A male fan-throated lizard shows off his throat flap to attract a female.

KOMODO DRAGON
HOW BIG: 2 to 3 m (6.6 to 9.8 ft) long
HOME: On and around Komodo Island in Asia
FOOD: Dead and live animals, from birds to horses

Its tongue helps taste, smell, and sense the location of far-away prey.

Surprising Skins

Many chameleons can change the pigmentation of their skin. Some camouflage themselves by matching the hues of plants. Many turn brighter to frighten other chameleons, then turn darker to show they give in.

Panther chameleons change shade depending on their mood.

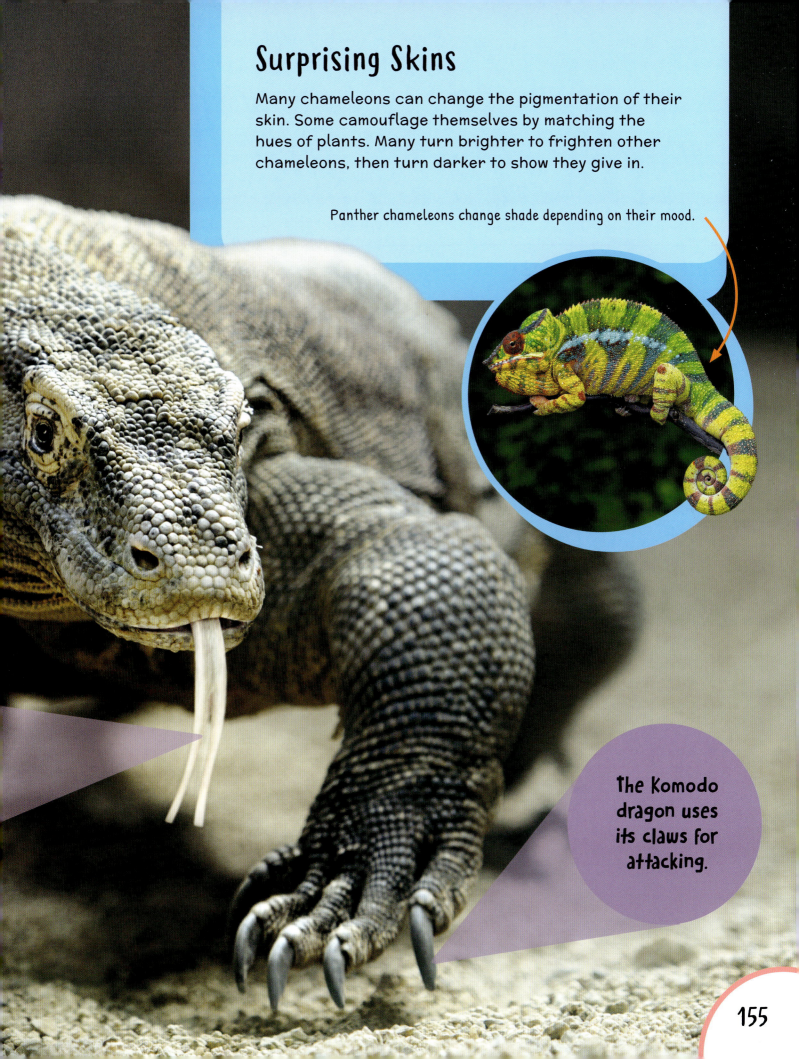

The Komodo dragon uses its claws for attacking.

TURTLES AND TORTOISES

The bodies of these reptiles are covered by a tough shell. Some, often called tortoises, live on land. Others live in oceans or lakes and ponds. They do not have teeth, so they chew with their hard, beaklike mouths.

The painted turtle spends most of the day basking.

Safe Shells

The bony shell is joined to the turtle's skeleton. It is usually covered by large, hard scales. One part of the shell covers the back, while the other part covers the belly. Many turtles can pull their head and legs inside their shell.

Galápagos giant tortoises have shells up to 1.5 m (4.9 ft) long.

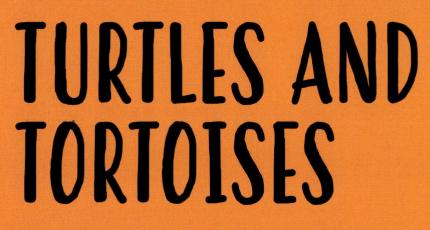

Sea Turtles

Sea turtles dive underwater to find seagrass, fish, or jellyfish. Like other reptiles, they need to breathe air, so they often come to the water surface. Female sea turtles bury their eggs on sandy beaches.

A sea turtle's four legs are shaped like flippers.

PAINTED TURTLE
HOW BIG: 7 to 25 cm
(3 to 10 in) long
HOME: Lakes and streams in
North America
FOOD: Plants, insects, and fish

In winter,
it digs into mud,
where it sleeps for
months without
breathing
or moving.

CROCODILES AND ALLIGATORS

Crocodiles and alligators are crocodilians. They have long snouts with big teeth—and powerful bites. They spend part of their time in water and part on land. Most live around rivers, lakes, and swamps, but some swim into seas.

A dwarf crocodile is 28 cm (11 in) long when it is born.

Crocodiles

Crocodiles live in tropical parts of the world. They have longer, narrower heads than alligators. When a crocodile's mouth is closed, all its teeth can still be seen. When an alligator's mouth is closed, only its top teeth can be seen.

The Nile crocodile attacks animals as big as zebras.

Alligators

The muscles that close an alligator's jaws are so strong it can hold tight to struggling prey. Yet the muscles that open an alligator's jaws are so weak that an adult human could hold them closed.

The American alligator lives in the southeastern United States.

DWARF CROCODILE
HOW BIG: 1.4 to 1.9 m (4.6 to 6.2 ft) long
HOME: Streams and swamps in Africa
FOOD: Fish, crabs, insects, and bats

After the dwarf crocodile hatches, its mother gently carries it to the water.

159

BIRDS

Birds have feathers and hard, toothless beaks. They have two legs for walking, with feet that are sometimes paddle-like for swimming or sharp-clawed for catching prey. All birds have wings, but not all birds can fly.

The hooded merganser duck can dive underwater as well as fly.

HOODED MERGANSER
HOW BIG: 40 to 49 cm
   (16 to 19 in) long
HOME: Ponds and wetlands
   in North America
FOOD: Fish, insects, and crabs

Feathers

Most birds have two types of feathers. Close to their skin are soft, warm feathers. Covering these are longer feathers that are waterproof, smooth, and strong. These outer feathers help birds flap through the air.

A peacock shows off his beautiful feathers to catch a female's eye.

Its beak has jagged edges for holding slippery fish.

Eggs

Female birds lay eggs with a hard shell. Until they hatch, eggs are kept safe and warm, often by parent birds sitting on them. Most birds lay their eggs in a nest. Nests can be in a tree hole or burrow, or made from twigs, mud, or spit.

Flamingos build their mud nests close together.

161

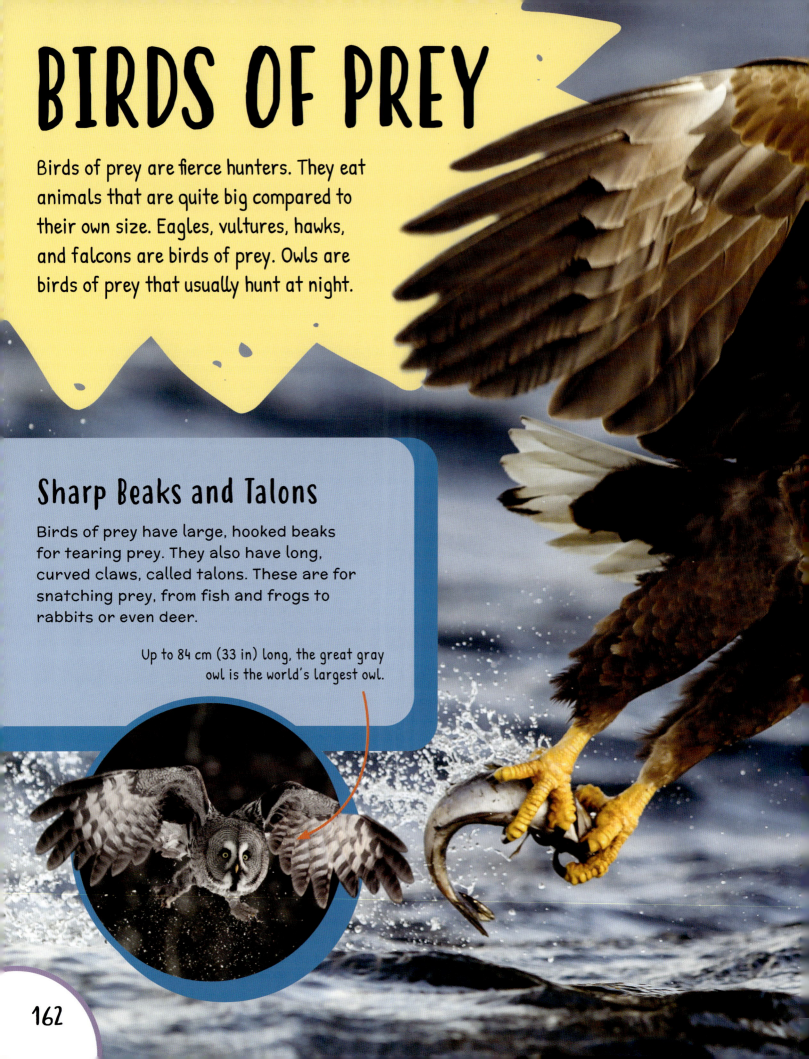

BIRDS OF PREY

Birds of prey are fierce hunters. They eat animals that are quite big compared to their own size. Eagles, vultures, hawks, and falcons are birds of prey. Owls are birds of prey that usually hunt at night.

Sharp Beaks and Talons

Birds of prey have large, hooked beaks for tearing prey. They also have long, curved claws, called talons. These are for snatching prey, from fish and frogs to rabbits or even deer.

Up to 84 cm (33 in) long, the great gray owl is the world's largest owl.

The white-tailed eagle has excellent eyesight.

Scavenging

Most birds of prey also eat dead animals they find. This is called scavenging. Vultures scavenge most of their food. They have nearly featherless heads and necks, so they do not get sticky feathers while feeding.

White-backed vultures often feed on dead zebras and warthogs.

WHITE-TAILED EAGLE
HOW BIG: 66 to 94 cm (26 to 37 in) long
HOME: Close to water in Europe and Asia
FOOD: Fish, birds, and dead animals

When spread wide, its wings are up to 2.4 m (8 ft) across.

HUMMINGBIRDS

These small birds live in the Americas. The bee hummingbird, which is 5 cm (2 in) long, is the world's smallest bird. To save energy, hummingbirds sleep so deeply that their heartbeats slow right down.

Anna's hummingbird has a straight, bendy beak.

Drinking Nectar

Hummingbirds eat insects and drink nectar. Nectar is a sugary liquid made inside flowers. To reach between flower petals, hummingbirds have long, thin beaks and even longer tongues.

Long-tailed sylphs can lick up nectar 13 times in a second.

ANNA'S HUMMINGBIRD
HOW BIG: 10 to 11 cm (4 to 4.3 in) long
HOME: Woodland and gardens
    in western North America
FOOD: Small insects and nectar

Its red throat sparkles in a rainbow of shades.

Humming

While they feed from flowers, hummingbirds hover with their wings flapping up to 90 times each second. This superfast movement makes a humming noise—and gives the birds their name.

The violet sabrewing flaps slower than most hummingbirds, making a lower hum.

EMUS AND OTHER RATITES

Ratites cannot fly. Emus, ostriches, and cassowaries are all ratites. Most ratites are very large and have long legs, making them fast runners. Ratites live in South America, Africa, and Australasia.

No Flying

Ratites have simpler wing bones and weaker wing muscles than other birds. Their feathers are also not suited to flying. They are soft and fluffy, so they cannot push against the air.

Found in Australia, the emu has small wings hidden by its feathers.

166

Sharp Claws

These birds run from danger, but big ratites can also give a nasty kick with their sharp-clawed feet. Cassowaries have the biggest claws of all birds, up to 12.5 cm (5 in) long.

Cassowaries grow a horny crest on their head.

The ostrich is the largest bird in the world.

OSTRICH
HOW BIG: 1.7 to 2.8 m (5.6 to 9.2 ft) tall
HOME: Grassland and desert in Africa
FOOD: Seeds, leaves, grass, and fruit

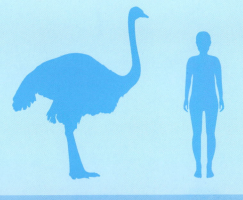

It can run at 70 km/h (43 miles per hour), faster than any other bird.

PENGUINS

Penguins have short wings, which cannot lift their chunky bodies into the air. Instead, penguins are strong swimmers. They spend most of their time at sea, but come on land to find a mate and lay eggs.

the emperor penguin lays just one egg each year.

EMPEROR PENGUIN
HOW BIG: 1.1 to 1.3 m (3.6 to 4.3 ft) tall
HOME: Ocean and floating ice around Antarctica
FOOD: Fish, krill, and squid

Super Swimmers

Penguin wings are shaped like flippers. They are used for pushing through the water while diving for food. Penguin toes are joined by skin, called webbing. Feet are used for paddling and steering.

Royal penguins catch fish and squid with their beaks.

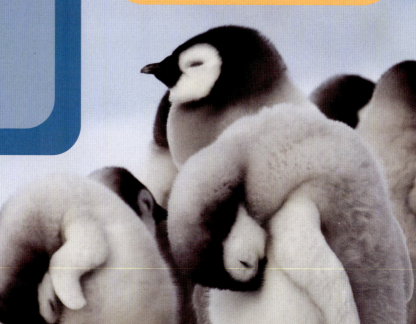

Keeping Warm

Most penguins live in cooler waters south of the equator. Some even swim in the icy water around Antarctica. To keep warm, they have a thick layer of fat. They can also puff up their feathers to keep out the wind.

An Adélie penguin warms an egg on its nest of stones in Antarctica.

A group of chicks is often looked after by one adult.

FISH

Fish live in salty seawater or in freshwater rivers and lakes. Most fish have scales, which are small, hard plates that grow from their skin. Fish swim by wriggling their bodies, tails, or fins. Fins are made of tough spines covered by skin.

The mandarinfish uses its large fins for steering.

Breathing Through Gills

Like all animals, fish need oxygen. We take oxygen from the air, but fish take it from water. They gulp water into their mouths. The water runs through their gills, where oxygen is soaked up. The used water flows out through gill slits.

A spotted eagle ray has five gill slits.

Surviving

Fish have many different ways to escape predators. Some fish with a large, muscly body can swim away fast. Camouflaged fish can hide. Fish that swim in a group, called a shoal, can keep watch together.

A porcupinefish swallows water so it blows up like a spiky balloon, making it too difficult to eat.

170

MANDARINFISH
HOW BIG: 5 to 7 cm
(2 to 2.8 in) long
HOME: Coral reefs in
the Pacific Ocean
FOOD: tiny invertebrates

Its pattern helps it hide on the bright coral reef.

SHARKS

There are over 400 species of sharks. The smallest is the dwarf lanternshark, which is 20 cm (8 in) long. The long whale shark is the biggest fish of all, at 12 m (40 ft) long. Unlike most fish, shark skeletons are made of bendy cartilage rather than bone.

Hunters

Most sharks hunt for prey using their excellent senses of smell, sight, and hearing. Sharks that eat big prey have many sharp teeth. Sharks that eat shellfish have flat teeth for cracking shells.

Hammerhead sharks have eyes at the sides of their T-shaped heads, so they can see all around.

A great white shark grows and loses 20,000 teeth in its life.

The dorsal (top) fin is large and triangular.

Gulpers

Whale, basking, and megamouth sharks do not use their tiny teeth for eating. Instead, they swim with their mouths open. As the water flows inside, tiny creatures are caught in net-like pads inside their mouths.

The whale shark's mouth is 1.5 m (4.9 ft) wide.

173

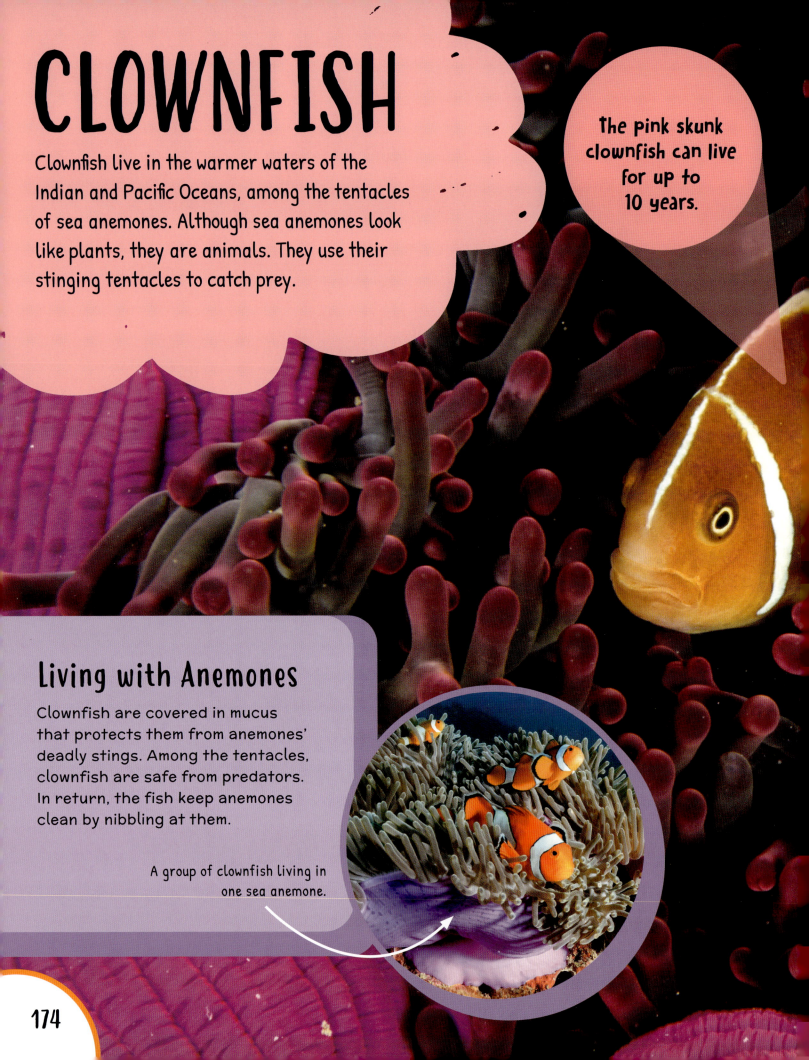

CLOWNFISH

Clownfish live in the warmer waters of the Indian and Pacific Oceans, among the tentacles of sea anemones. Although sea anemones look like plants, they are animals. They use their stinging tentacles to catch prey.

The pink skunk clownfish can live for up to 10 years.

Living with Anemones

Clownfish are covered in mucus that protects them from anemones' deadly stings. Among the tentacles, clownfish are safe from predators. In return, the fish keep anemones clean by nibbling at them.

A group of clownfish living in one sea anemone.

A sea anemone's tentacles wave around its mouth.

Unusual Parents

All clownfish are born male. In each group of fish, the biggest male turns into a female. After she has laid up to 1,500 eggs, a male clownfish guards them until they hatch.

A male saddleback clownfish takes care of his group's red eggs, which have been laid on the seafloor.

PINK SKUNK CLOWNFISH
HOW BIG: 4 to 10 cm (1.6 to 4 in) long
HOME: Sea anemones in the Indian and Pacific Oceans
FOOD: Plant-like algae and tiny invertebrates

ANGLERFISH

On an anglerfish's head is a long growth, shaped like a fishing rod. At its end is a "lure" that looks like a little animal. The anglerfish wiggles the lure to attract prey, which it then sucks into its large mouth.

Making Light

In the dark of the deep ocean, some anglerfish use light to attract prey. The lure at the end of their fishing rod has tiny light-making bacteria. These make the lure glow.

This whipnose anglerfish is attracting a fish with its glowing lure.

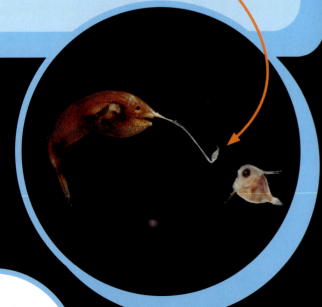

The painted frogfish's lure looks like a fish.

Its mouth opens wide for catching prey as big as the frogfish itself.

PAINTED FROGFISH
HOW BIG: 15 to 30 cm (6 to 12 in) long
HOME: Around sponges in the Indian and Pacific Oceans
FOOD: Fish, shrimps, and crabs

Clinging On

In some anglerfish species, males are much smaller than females and cannot survive without them. Males must attach themselves to a female and be fed by her blood.

A male headlight anglerfish clings to a female with his teeth.

SEAHORSES

Seahorses live in shallow seawater, where they hide among coral, seagrass, or plant roots. They are covered in bony plates, which make their bodies stiff. Unlike most fish, they swim upright, wafting slowly along with their fins.

The pygmy seahorse is well camouflaged among coral.

Egg Pouch

Most fish lay eggs and then swim away, but seahorses keep their eggs safe. Females lay their eggs in a pouch on a male's front. After the eggs hatch, the male squeezes, and pushes out his babies.

A male lined seahorse gives birth to up to 650 babies.

PYGMY SEAHORSE
HOW BIG: 1.7 to 2 cm
(0.7 to 0.8 in) long
HOME: Soft corals in the Indian and Pacific Oceans
FOOD: tiny invertebrates

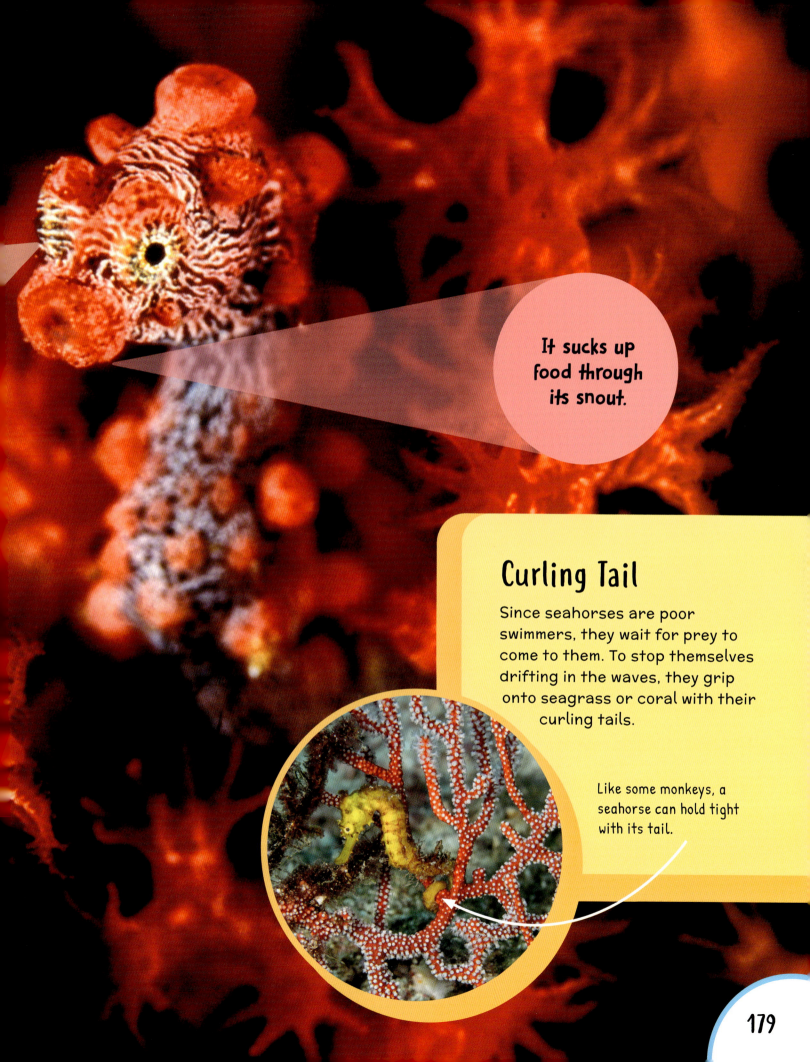

It sucks up food through its snout.

Curling Tail

Since seahorses are poor swimmers, they wait for prey to come to them. To stop themselves drifting in the waves, they grip onto seagrass or coral with their curling tails.

Like some monkeys, a seahorse can hold tight with its tail.

GOURAMIS

Gouramis take oxygen from the water using their gills, but they can also breathe oxygen from air. This is useful in the shallow, slow-moving ponds and lakes where they live, as the water contains very little oxygen.

Bubble Nests

Most male gouramis make nests of bubbles that they blow with their mouths. When the female lays her eggs, the male takes them to the nest in his mouth.

A male betta guards his nest, where tiny babies are floating until they can swim alone.

These long fins can feel the way in muddy water.

The dwarf gourami often gulps air at the water's surface.

DWARF GOURAMI
HOW BIG: 5 to 9 cm (2 to 3.5 in) long
HOME: Ponds, swamps, and ditches in Asia
FOOD: Algae and small invertebrates

Kissing

Kissing gourami fish have sticking-out lips that are lined with teeth. These lips are good at scraping up algae to eat. When fighting, a gourami presses its lips against the other fish, trying to push it through the water.

These kissing gourami fish are fighting, not being friendly.

AMPHIBIANS

Frogs and toads belong to a family called amphibians. Most amphibians lay their jelly-like eggs in freshwater. Young amphibians live in water, but most adults can crawl or hop onto land.

The cane toad is the world's largest toad.

Metamorphosis

Young amphibians, called larvae, have gills so they can breathe in water (see page 170). As larvae grow, their body shape changes, and they develop lungs to breathe air. This change is called metamorphosis.

After hatching from its egg (left), a salamander larva (right) lives in water.

Moist Skin

Amphibians also soak up oxygen through their thin skin. Their skin can breathe only if it is damp, so amphibians make slimy mucus to stop it drying out.

Caecilians are legless amphibians that live in hot, wet places.

CANE TOAD
HOW BIG: 10 to 24 cm
(4 to 9.4 in) long
HOME: Central to South
America and Australasia
FOOD: Insects, lizards, and mice

Toads are part of the frog family. They have drier, bumpier skin.

FROGS

Frog larvae are called tadpoles. They hatch from their eggs in a puddle or pond. Adult frogs live on land or in freshwater. On land, they stay close to water, or live in rainy places so they do not dry out.

These green flying frogs live in tall trees.

Sticky Tongue

Little frogs eat insects like flies and moths. They catch them with their sticky tongues. Some big frogs can catch mice or bats, which they shove into their mouths with their hands.

Frogs dart out their long tongues to catch fast-moving flies.

Tadpoles

Tadpoles have no arms and legs, so they swim by wriggling their tail. After a few weeks or months, they lose their tail and grow legs for hopping or swimming.

This poison dart frog is carrying a tadpole to a new pool.

They can make big jumps with their long, strong back legs.

GREEN FLYING FROG
HOW BIG: 4 to 8 cm (1.5 to 3 in) long
HOME: Rain forests in Asia
FOOD: Insects and spiders

SALAMANDERS

Most adult salamanders have four short legs and a tail. They live on land, in water, or in both. Unlike most amphibians, some water-living salamanders keep their gills throughout their life.

This adult's feathery gills take oxygen from the water.

Living in a Cave

Some salamanders live in dark caves. Many of them are blind, but have excellent senses of hearing and smell. Some cave salamanders are pigmentless, but darken if they are taken outside.

Found in underground rivers, the olm is eyeless. It keeps its pink gills as an adult.

Don't Eat Me

Salamander skins ooze a liquid that tastes nasty and is sometimes poisonous. The bright shades of their skin warn predators that they are bad to eat.

Once a predator has tasted a fire salamander, it will remember that black and yellow animals are bad to eat!

AXOLOTL
HOW BIG: 15 to 45 cm
(6 to 18 in) long
HOME: Lake Xochimilco in Mexico
FOOD: Fish, insects, and worms

The axolotl sucks prey into its mouth.

INVERTEBRATES

Invertebrate means "without a backbone." Most animals are invertebrates. There are at least 1,500,000 species of invertebrates, but only 60,000 other animal species. Invertebrates come in many shapes and sizes. They swim, fly, walk, jump, or stay still.

No Bones

Invertebrates have no bony skeleton inside their bodies. Some have soft bodies, such as jellyfish or slugs. Others have a hard covering called an exoskeleton.

A centipede has an exoskeleton and lots of legs.

Insects

Insects are the largest group of invertebrates. An exoskeleton covers their body, which is in three parts: head, thorax, and abdomen. They have six legs, plus two feelers, called antennae, on their head.

A praying mantis uses four legs for walking and two for catching prey.

The crimson dropwing dragonfly is an insect.

Like many insects, it has two pairs of wings.

CRIMSON DROPWING
HOW BIG: 3 to 3.5 cm (1.2 to 1.4 in) long
HOME: Around ponds and streams in Asia
FOOD: Small insects

OCTOPUSES

Octopuses live in the ocean. They have soft bodies, with eight arms for grabbing food and crawling. They swim by squeezing out a jet of water, pushing themselves in the opposite direction.

The wunderpus changes its pigmentation pattern for camouflage.

WUNDERPUS
HOW BIG: 20 to 25 cm (8 to 10 in) long
HOME: Shallows of the Indian and Pacific Oceans
FOOD: Shrimps, shellfish, and fish

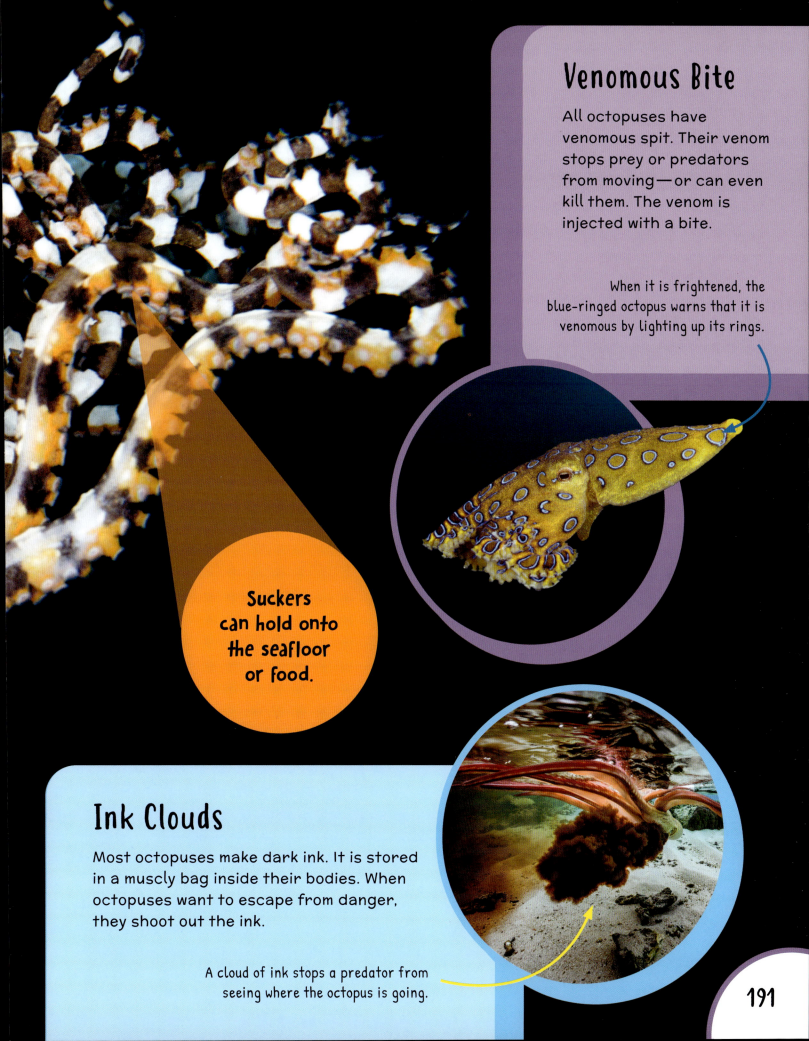

Venomous Bite

All octopuses have venomous spit. Their venom stops prey or predators from moving—or can even kill them. The venom is injected with a bite.

When it is frightened, the blue-ringed octopus warns that it is venomous by lighting up its rings.

Suckers can hold onto the seafloor or food.

Ink Clouds

Most octopuses make dark ink. It is stored in a muscly bag inside their bodies. When octopuses want to escape from danger, they shoot out the ink.

A cloud of ink stops a predator from seeing where the octopus is going.

191

JELLYFISH

A jellyfish has a soft, umbrella-shaped body called a bell. Its tentacles have stingers that kill or stun prey. Food is then pulled to the jellyfish's mouth or mouths, on the inside of the bell.

The fried egg jellyfish's bell looks like ... a fried egg!

FRIED EGG JELLYFISH
HOW BIG: 15 to 40 cm
(6 to 18 in) long
HOME: Mediterranean Sea
FOOD: tiny animals and other small living things

It does not have a brain or eyes, but it can feel its surroundings.

Changing Body

A jellyfish starts life as a round larva, floating in the ocean. The larva sticks itself to a rock. Then it grows into a flower-shaped creature called a polyp. After a while, bits of the polyp break off, then grow into adult, umbrella-shaped jellyfish.

Polyps have tentacles for catching food and mouths for eating and pooping.

Squeezing Along

An adult jellyfish swims by squeezing the muscles in its bell, closing it a little, then relaxing. This pushes water behind the jellyfish, driving it forward.

These jellyfish are swimming in a group, called a swarm.

STARFISH

Starfish live on the seafloor. They crawl using suckers, called tube feet, on the underside of their arms. Tube feet can stick to rocks or coral. Most starfish have five arms, but some have over 50.

Inside-Out Stomach

A starfish's mouth is on its underside. When a starfish finds prey, it pushes its stomach out through its mouth, inside out. The stomach and food are pulled inside the starfish.

This blue starfish is eating algae with its stomach, which is 4 cm (1.6 in) long.

It has protection made of bony plates.

Arm Growing

Many starfish can grow a new arm if one is lost. Some starfish can even regrow their whole body from just one arm.

A new six-armed Luzon starfish is regrowing from one arm.

NECKLACE STARFISH
HOW BIG: 15 to 30 cm
(6 to 12 in) long
HOME: Coral reefs in the
Indian and Pacific Oceans
FOOD: Sponges and algae

The necklace starfish has hundreds of tube feet.

BEETLES

Beetles live almost everywhere on Earth, apart from the icy poles and the oceans. These insects are very common. Of around 1,000,000 species of insects, about 400,000 are beetles.

This male dung beetle has rolled a ball of animal poop.

Wings

Most beetles have two pairs of wings. Their front wings are hard and cannot be used to fly. They are covers for the delicate back wings, which most beetles use for flying.

A ladybird or ladybug lifts its front wings and opens its flight wings.

AFRICAN DUNG BEETLE
HOW BIG: 2.5 to 5 cm
(1 to 2 in) long
HOME: Grassland in Africa
FOOD: Poop from mammals

A female beetle will lay eggs in the ball.

Biting Jaws

Beetles have strong jaws for grabbing and chewing their food. Two jaws, called mandibles, stick out on either side of their mouth, looking a bit like scissor blades.

Male stag beetles use their huge mandibles for fighting.

197

BEES AND WASPS

These insects hatch from their eggs as legless larvae. During a resting stage, called pupation, they turn into winged adults. Some female bees and wasps can sting by injecting venom through a tube at the tip of their abdomen.

Living Together

Some bees and wasps live in large groups, sharing a nest. Female workers collect food and look after the group's larvae. Only one large female, the queen, can lay eggs. Some eggs hatch into males, who fly off to mate with other queens.

This paper wasp queen is building a nest from plant stems and spit.

Living Alone

Many bees and wasps live alone. All the females can lay their own eggs. Some make their own nests, while others lay eggs in the nests of different species.

A ruby-tailed wasp is hoping to lay eggs in a potter wasp's nest.

It carries pollen to the nest in baskets on its back legs.

WESTERN HONEY BEE
HOW BIG: 1 to 2 cm (0.4 to 0.8 in) long
HOME: Everywhere with flowering plants
FOOD: Flower nectar and pollen

The western honey bee makes honey from flower nectar.

ANTS

Ants are in the same group of insects as bees and wasps. Like them, ants have a narrow "waist" in the middle of their abdomen. Ants live in groups called colonies. Sometimes, colonies contain millions of ants!

WEAVER ANT
HOW BIG: 0.5 to 2.5 cm (0.2 to 1 in) long
HOME: trees in Asia and Australia
FOOD: Insects and their sweet sap

The leaves will be stitched together with silk made by larvae.

Communication

Ants can "talk" to each other by touching, often by tapping with their antennae. They also make smelly chemicals, which they use to mark trails between their nest and food.

Army ants are following a trail as they carry larvae to a new nest.

Weaver ant workers are using their mandibles to build a nest.

Different Jobs

Most ants in a colony are female. They do different jobs and have bodies suited to their work. For example, there are large egg-laying queens, small workers, and large-jawed soldiers.

This honey ant's job is to be fed until its abdomen swells with sweet liquid. When other ants are hungry, it spits some up.

SLUGS AND SNAILS

Slugs and snails are gastropods. They live in freshwater, in oceans, and on land. When they have a shell, and can pull their soft body inside it, they are called snails. Gastropods without a shell are called slugs.

These wavy strands soak up oxygen from the water.

PINK SEA SLUG
HOW BIG: 2 to 5 cm (0.8 to 2 in) long
HOME: Shallows of the Atlantic Ocean
FOOD: Invertebrates

A pink sea slug's bright pigmentation warns predators that it tastes nasty.

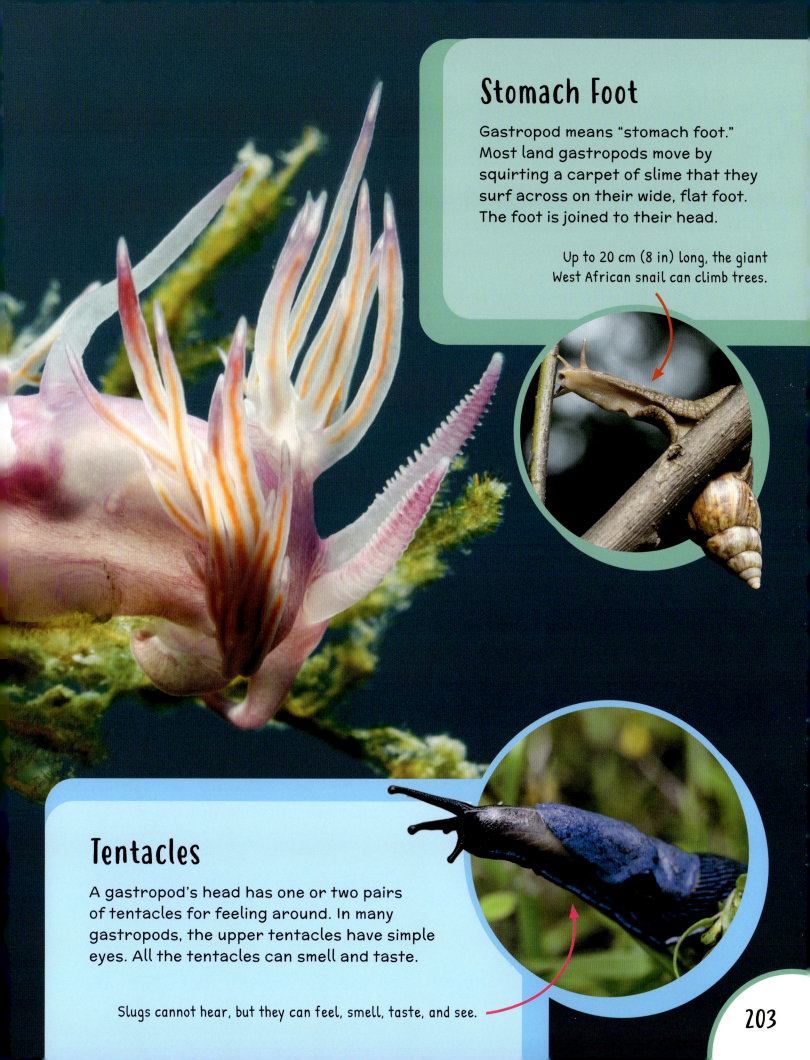

Stomach Foot

Gastropod means "stomach foot." Most land gastropods move by squirting a carpet of slime that they surf across on their wide, flat foot. The foot is joined to their head.

Up to 20 cm (8 in) long, the giant West African snail can climb trees.

Tentacles

A gastropod's head has one or two pairs of tentacles for feeling around. In many gastropods, the upper tentacles have simple eyes. All the tentacles can smell and taste.

Slugs cannot hear, but they can feel, smell, taste, and see.

SPIDERS

Like insects, spiders have exoskeletons. Unlike insects, they have eight legs and their bodies are in two parts. The front part contains a spider's brain and stomach.

A jumping spider has two main eyes, plus six smaller ones.

Fangs

Above its mouth, a spider has a pair of mouthparts that end in a sharp, hollow fang. When a spider bites, venom runs through its fangs and into prey. The venom kills prey, or stops it moving.

A tarantula folds out its fangs when it wants to bite.

These feelers, called pedipalps, can hold food.

Catching Prey

Spiders usually eat insects or other invertebrates. Some spiders chase prey or jump out on it. Others build traps, called webs, from silk that they make in their body.

The trapdoor spider makes a burrow, attaching an earth door with silk. When prey comes past, the spider leaps out.

HEAVY JUMPING SPIDER
HOW BIG: 1 to 2.5 cm (0.4 to 1 in) long
HOME: Grassland and forests in Asia
FOOD: Small insects

SCORPIONS

Like spiders, scorpions are arachnids. They have eight legs, plus a pair of pincers for grabbing prey. Their bodies have two eyes on top, and four to 10 eyes along their edges.

Sting in the Tail

Scorpions have tails that are in five parts. Venom is made in the last part. This part ends in a sharp, curved stinger. The stinger pricks prey, then injects venom.

Hairs on the tail can feel prey, which helps the scorpion guide its stinger.

It crushes prey with its pincers.

The fat-tailed scorpion makes very dangerous venom.

Piggybacking

Female scorpions give birth to babies rather than laying eggs. At first, babies are carried on their mother's back. As they grow, they shed their hard exoskeleton when it gets tight. Underneath is a softer one that slowly hardens.

A mother scorpion protects her babies.

DINOSAURS

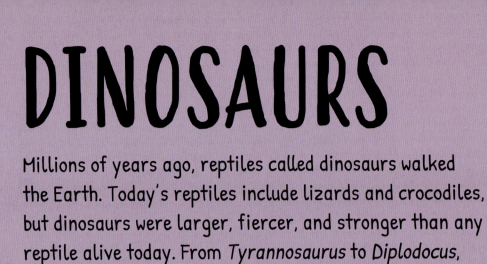

Millions of years ago, reptiles called dinosaurs walked the Earth. Today's reptiles include lizards and crocodiles, but dinosaurs were larger, fiercer, and stronger than any reptile alive today. From *Tyrannosaurus* to *Diplodocus*, find out about the amazing dinosaurs.

Meat-Eating Dinosaurs

Little meat-eating dinosaurs chased insects or frogs. Big meat-eaters used sharp teeth and claws to kill other dinosaurs, fish, or mammals.

The Asian dinosaur *Ichthyovenator* ate fish and flying reptiles.

Acrocanthosaurus was a meat-eating dinosaur 11 m (36 ft) long.

Plant-Eating Dinosaurs

Plant-eaters fed on leaves, fruits, or nuts. Every plant-eater needed to escape the jaws of meat-eaters. Some ran away fast, while others were too big or spiky to be eaten.

Gigantspinosaurus had long spikes on its shoulders, which made it hard to capture.

Like all dinosaurs, it had four limbs.

Flying and Swimming Reptiles

While dinosaurs stomped or scampered across the land, other reptiles flew through the air on wide wings. In the oceans, swimming reptiles snapped up fish, squid, or each other.

Flying reptiles had wings up to 11 m (36 ft) wide.

DIFFERENT DINOSAURS

Dinosaurs were a group of reptiles that evolved around 233 million years ago. Their skeletons had important differences when compared with the bones of other reptiles. These differences gave dinosaurs advantages that made them very successful for millions of years.

Coelophysis was one of the earliest dinosaurs.

Stand Up Straight!

Unlike other reptiles, dinosaurs walked with their back legs beneath their body rather than sprawled to the sides. This meant they could run faster.

A lizard's legs stretch out to the sides of its body, but a dinosaur's strong legs were directly beneath its body.

Like all early dinosaurs, it ran on its back legs.

Super Skulls

Dinosaur teeth were fixed deep in their jaws, so they were less likely to fall out when biting prey. Their skulls also had several extra holes that made them lighter but not weaker.

A *Tyrannosaurus* skull had holes in front of and behind its eyes.

COELOPHYSIS (see-loh-FISE-iss)
HOW BIG: 2 to 3 m (7 to 10 ft) long
HOME: Plains in North America and Africa
FOOD: Lizards and other small animals
WHEN: 216 to 196 million years ago

SCALES AND FEATHERS

Early dinosaurs had skin covered by scales. A few million years later, some meat-eating dinosaurs started to grow feathers. Scales and feathers are made of the same hard material that is in human hair and nails. Scales are usually flat, while feathers are long and branching.

Citipati was a feathered dinosaur that could not fly.

Strong Scales

Most dinosaurs had scales. Scales are small plates that grow from skin, protecting it from damage. Scientists have tested fossilized scales to find out what shade they were.

While some dinosaurs were brown or green, others were brightly patterned!

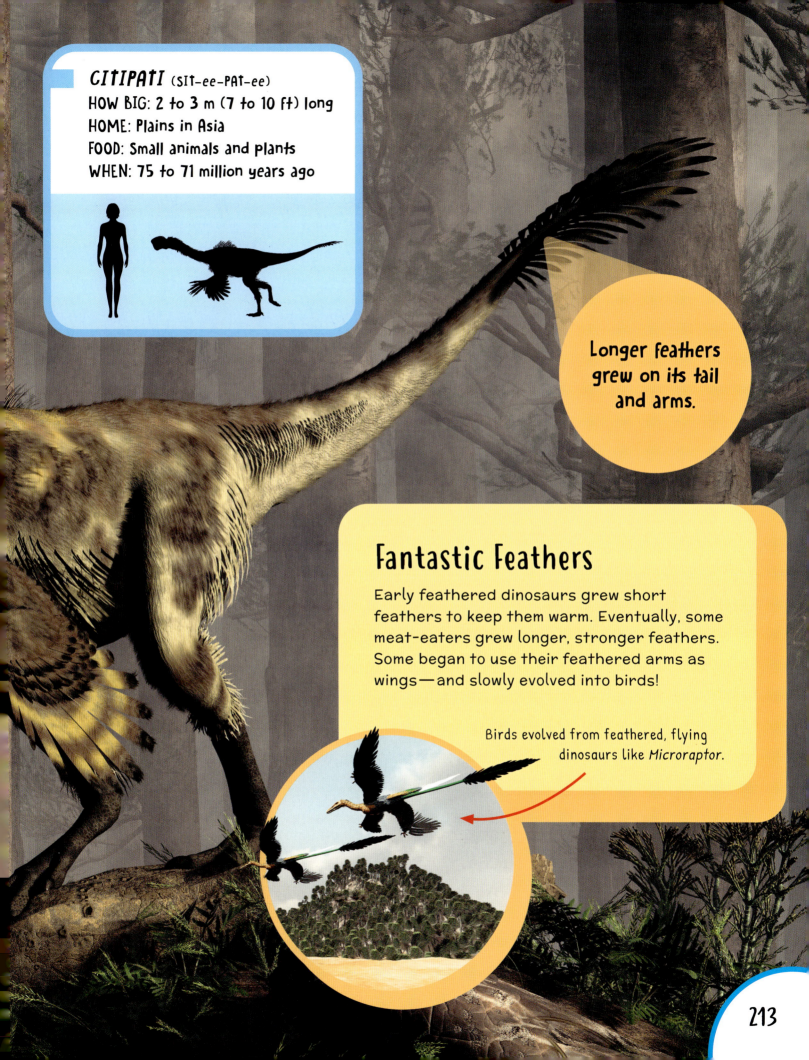

Longer feathers grew on its tail and arms.

Fantastic Feathers

Early feathered dinosaurs grew short feathers to keep them warm. Eventually, some meat-eaters grew longer, stronger feathers. Some began to use their feathered arms as wings—and slowly evolved into birds!

Birds evolved from feathered, flying dinosaurs like *Microraptor*.

FAST AND SLOW

We can make guesses about how fast dinosaurs walked and ran by looking at their leg bones and measuring their footprints. The fastest dinosaurs could run more quickly than any human adult, while the slowest dinosaurs could have been outrun by a human child.

Slowest

Large plant-eaters weighed up to 100 tonnes (110 tons), as much as 50 family cars. They had to walk slowly on their four thick legs. Adults had no need to run, as their size kept them safe from meat-eaters.

Brachiosaurus's legs were suited to holding its great weight, rather than to sprinting.

VELOCIRAPTOR
(veh-LOSS-ee-rap-tuhr)
HOW BIG: 1 to 2 m (3 to 7 ft) long
HOME: Dry plains in Asia
FOOD: Small reptiles, amphibians, and mammals
WHEN: 75 to 71 million years ago

Fastest

Slim meat-eaters, such as *Gallimimus*, were the fastest runners. They ran on their back legs. Like today's ostriches, their legs were long and muscly. It is possible that some of these dinosaurs could have run as fast as ostriches: 72 km/h (45 miles per hour).

Gallimimus used its long tail for balance as it ran.

Small meat-eaters used speed to catch prey.

Velociraptor could have reached speeds up to 40 km/h (25 miles per hour).

MEAT-EATING DINOSAURS

Meat-eating dinosaurs had sharp teeth and claws for catching and chewing their food. Some meat-eaters ate dinosaurs, but others ate fish, lizards, or insects. While the biggest, fiercest meat-eaters reached 16 m (52 ft) long, the smallest were only 34 cm (1 ft) long.

GIGANOTOSAURUS (jig-an-OH-toe-SORE-us)
HOW BIG: 12 to 13 m (39 to 47 ft) long
HOME: Swamps in South America
FOOD: Plant-eating dinosaurs
WHEN: 98 to 97 million years ago

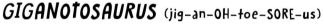

Most theropods had much shorter front limbs than back limbs.

Dinosaur Diet

Around 233 million years ago, the earliest dinosaurs were meat-eaters. Over millions of years, some dinosaurs evolved (or slowly changed) to eat plants. Of all the dinosaurs we know, around one-third were meat-eaters, while two-thirds were plant-eaters.

Feathery *Anchiornis* was one of the smallest meat-eaters. It ate lizards and fish.

Giganotosaurus's long tail helped it to balance on its back legs.

Theropods

All the meat-eating dinosaurs belonged to a group of similar dinosaurs called theropods. Theropod means "beast foot" in ancient Greek. Theropods walked on their back legs. Most big theropods had scaly skin, but some smaller theropods had feathers.

Like most theropods, *Megaraptor* had three main fingers and three main toes.

ALLOSAURUS

This large meat-eater had up to 44 sharp teeth with jagged edges. These teeth sometimes fell out as *Allosaurus* ripped through flesh, so they are common fossils. *Allosaurus* bite marks have been found in dinosaurs as large as *Stegosaurus*.

Its short horns might have been helpful for bashing other *Allosauruses*.

Killer Claws

Each hand had three fingers, armed with long, curved claws. *Allosaurus* could not reach forward easily with its short arms. However, once prey was in its mouth, the hook-like claws stopped escape.

An *Allosaurus* claw could grow over 18 cm (7 in) long.

218

ALLOSAURUS (AL-oh-SORE-us)
HOW BIG: 8 to 12 m (26 to 39 ft) long
HOME: Forests and plains in North
America and Europe
FOOD: Large plant-eating dinosaurs
WHEN: 155 to 145 million years ago

Allosauruses may have worked as a team to hunt big prey.

Growing Up

Allosaurus reached its full size by around 15 years old. Every year as it grew, it gained around 150 kg (330 lb)—the weight of 40 human babies. Most Allosauruses lived to be around 25.

Allosaurus was big enough to attack young or sick Diplodocuses.

219

SPINOSAURUS

Spinosaurus was one of the biggest meat-eaters that ever lived. Its long, narrow skull looked rather like a modern crocodile's. This dinosaur used the long claws on its thumbs, as well as its sharp teeth, to grab slippery fish.

Spinosaurus's teeth grew up to 15 cm (6 in) long.

SPINOSAURUS (SPINE-oh-SORE-us)
HOW BIG: 12 to 16 m (39 to 52 ft) long
HOME: Around water in North Africa
FOOD: Fish, dinosaurs, and flying reptiles
WHEN: 112 to 93 million years ago

Strange Sail

Bony spines grew from *Spinosaurus*'s back. These were covered by skin, making a "sail." *Spinosaurus* may have shown off its sail to attract a mate. Today, peacocks use their long tails in the same way.

The spines on *Spinosaurus*'s back were up to 1.6 m (5.4 ft) long.

Its strong back legs were suited to wading.

Super Swimmer

Unlike most dinosaurs, *Spinosaurus* spent a lot of time in rivers and shallow seas. Its long, paddle-shaped tail could have powered it through the water.

Spinosaurus tries to snap up an *Onchopristis* fish.

TYRANNOSAURUS

Tyrannosaurus was the biggest meat-eater that ever lived in North America. An adult *Tyrannosaurus* had no need to fear any other animal. However, this deadly beast was wiped out when a giant space rock hit Earth, around 66 million years ago.

Powerful Bite

Tyrannosaurus had one of the strongest bites of any animal that has ever lived. Its bite force was equal to the weight of three small cars. Its thick, strong jaw bones could open very wide, before powerful muscles snapped them closed.

Tyrannosaurus's jaws could crush bone.

TYRANNOSAURUS (ty-RAN-oh-SORE-us)
HOW BIG: 11 to 12 m (36 to 40 ft) long
HOME: Swamps and forests in North America
FOOD: Plant-eating dinosaurs, found alive or already dead
WHEN: 68 to 66 million years ago

Tyrannosaurus's knife-like teeth grew over 30 cm (12 in) long.

Sense of Smell

Like modern meat-eaters, from great white sharks to wolves, *Tyrannosaurus* had a very good sense of smell. The part of its brain that made sense of smells was also large.

Tyrannosaurus's sense of smell enabled it to track plant-eating dinosaurs for many miles.

Their short arms had only two clawed fingers.

ARCHAEOPTERYX

Over millions of years, some dinosaurs grew to look more and more like birds. By 150 million years ago, dinosaurs like *Archaeopteryx* could use their feathered arms to make short flights. By 130 million years ago, the first true birds had evolved from their dinosaur grandparents.

Dinosaur or Bird?

Archaeopteryx had features of both dinosaurs and birds. Like most dinosaurs, but unlike modern birds, it had teeth. However, its arm muscles and bones had evolved into wide wings.

Archaeopteryx used its sharp little teeth for snapping up insects.

Its bony tail was much longer than a modern bird's.

ARCHAEOPTERYX (ARK-ee-OPT-er-ix)
HOW BIG: 30 to 50 cm (12 to 20 in) long
HOME: Islands in Europe
FOOD: Insects and other small animals
WHEN: 150 to 148 million years ago

Unlike today's birds, Archaeopteryx had clawed fingers.

Dinosaurs Are Alive!

After a space rock hit Earth 66 million years ago, all the dinosaurs died out—apart from the dinosaurs that had evolved into birds. Today's birds are the closest living relatives of *Tyrannosaurus*.

Hesperornis was a toothed bird that lived 83 to 78 million years ago.

PLANT-EATING DINOSAURS

The biggest plant-eaters were 40 m (131 ft) long, but the littlest were only dog-sized. Some walked on two legs and others on four. Many had long necks, but others had bony plates. Plant-eaters developed different body shapes in order to find food and defend themselves against hungry meat-eaters.

Kosmoceratops had more horns than any animal that ever lived.

Telling Teeth

Fossils of plant-eaters' teeth tell us what they ate. Some dinosaurs had thin teeth for stripping soft fern leaves. Others had wide, spoon-shaped teeth for ripping tough twigs.

Edmontosaurus had a hard, toothless beak for clipping stems, plus hundreds of small teeth at the back of its mouth for grinding.

It cut through stems with its hard, horny beak.

Precious Plant-Eaters

More dinosaurs ate plants than ate meat. Today, there are more plant-eating animals than meat-eaters, too. If there were more meat-eaters, there would soon be no animals left for them to eat!

A pack of meat-eaters corners a frightened plant-eating *Einiosaurus*.

KOSMOCERATOPS (KOZ-mo-SEH-ra-tops)
HOW BIG: 4 to 5 m (13 to 16 ft) long
HOME: Forests in North America
FOOD: Woody plants
WHEN: 76 to 75 million years ago

DIPLODOCUS

The huge size of this peaceful dinosaur protected it from attack. Even the largest local meat-eaters, *Allosaurus* and *Ceratosaurus*, could not kill an adult *Diplodocus*. This dinosaur was part of the sauropod group of plant-eaters, which had long necks and long tails.

Diplodocus's neck was over 6 m (20 ft) long.

Feeding High and Low

Its long neck enabled *Diplodocus* to feed on low plants a distance away, saving the energy needed to walk toward them. It could also rear up on its back legs to reach branches up to 11 m (36 ft) high.

Diplodocus's long neck meant it did not have to compete with most other plant-eaters for food.

DIPLODOCUS (dip-LOH-doh-kus)
HOW BIG: 24 to 32 m (79 to 105 ft) long
HOME: Plains in North America
FOOD: Soft leaves
WHEN: 154 to 152 million years ago

Cracking a Whip

Diplodocus's tail grew to 14 m (46 ft) long. Made of 80 small bones, it was very bendy. The dinosaur could crack it like a whip, making a sudden loud noise that frightened away predators.

Diplodocus's tail was longer than the longest buses we have today.

Four thick legs supported its 18-tonne (20-ton) weight.

ARGENTINOSAURUS

Argentinosaurus was probably the biggest land animal that ever lived. It reached over 39 m (128 ft) long, which is longer than eight cars. Like *Diplodocus*, *Argentinosaurus* was a long-necked, long-tailed sauropod. It was one of the slowest moving of all the dinosaurs.

Staying Safe

Fossilized footprints show us that sauropods often moved in herds. Young dinosaurs walked in the middle to stay safe from attack. It took around 30 years for a newborn *Argentinosaurus*, just 1 m (3 ft) long at birth, to reach full size.

Argentinosaurus herds may have migrated in search of food and water.

Argentinosaurus's skin was covered by small scales.

Its skull was small enough to be held up by its slim neck.

ARGENTINOSAURUS

(AR–juhn–TEE–no–SORE–us)

HOW BIG: 30 to 39 m (98 to 128 ft) long
HOME: Plains in South America
FOOD: Leaves of conifer trees
WHEN: 96 to 92 million years ago

Wait for It...

This dinosaur's size gave room for a huge stomach and long intestines, which are tubes where food is broken down. It took two weeks for plants to travel through this dinosaur's body, giving it extra time to soak up the plants' goodness.

Fossilized dinosaur poop is called coprolite.

TRICERATOPS

Triceratops had a horned face and a bone frill that jutted over its neck. These features were probably little help in battles against large local meat-eaters like *Tyrannosaurus*. Yet, weighing more than seven family cars, *Triceratops* could have charged at its attackers.

Its horns were shown off to impress other *Triceratops*.

Three Horns

Triceratops means "three-horned face." A horn, 1 m (3 ft) long, was above each eye, while a shorter horn decorated the snout. These horns might have frightened small meat-eaters, but they were not sharp or strong enough to be very useful weapons.

Bite marks on *Triceratops* bones tell us the plant-eater lost battles against *Tyrannosaurus*.

Weighing In

With its great weight, *Triceratops* could not reach high to feed. Yet it may have used its weight and horns to knock over shrubs and trees. It gripped plants with its hard beak, then mashed them with its back teeth.

Triceratops's skull, up to 2.5 m (8.2 ft) long, was among the largest of all land animals.

TRICERATOPS (try-SEH-ra-tops)
HOW BIG: 8 to 9 m (26 to 30 ft) long
HOME: Forests and plains in North America
FOOD: tough plants
WHEN: 68 to 66 million years ago

Its four broad toes were shaped like hooves.

STEGOSAURUS

This plant-eater had two rows of kite-shaped plates down its back. Their pattern may have helped *Stegosaurus* recognize other members of its herd from a distance. *Stegosaurus* had a small brain, suiting this dinosaur to a slow and simple life.

STEGOSAURUS (STEG-oh-SORE-us)
HOW BIG: 7 to 9 m (23 to 30 ft) long
HOME: Forest and plains in
North America and Europe
FOOD: Low plants
WHEN: 155 to 150 million years ago

The tail spikes were up to 90 cm (35 in) long.

Terrible Thagomizer

The tip of *Stegosaurus*'s tail had four sharp spikes. When whipped at an attacker, these made deep wounds. This type of tail was named a "thagomizer" by a cartoonist named Gary Larson.

With a flick of its tail, a stegosaur escapes.

234

The plates were too thin be used to protect *Stegosaurus*.

Scales vs. Plates

Unlike scales, which grow from the top layer of an animal's skin, *Stegosaurus*'s back plates grew from deep inside its skin. Scales are made from keratin, like claws, while plates are made from bone.

Stegosaurus's biggest plates were 60 cm (24 in) tall.

ANKYLOSAURUS

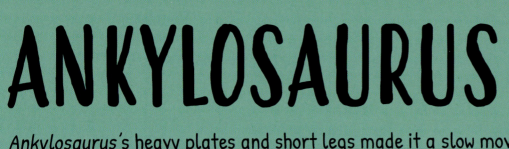

Ankylosaurus's heavy plates and short legs made it a slow mover. This tank-like dinosaur was a close relative of the nodosaurs. Yet *Ankylosaurus* had a terrifying weapon that nodosaurs did not possess: a hard, heavy club at the end of its tail.

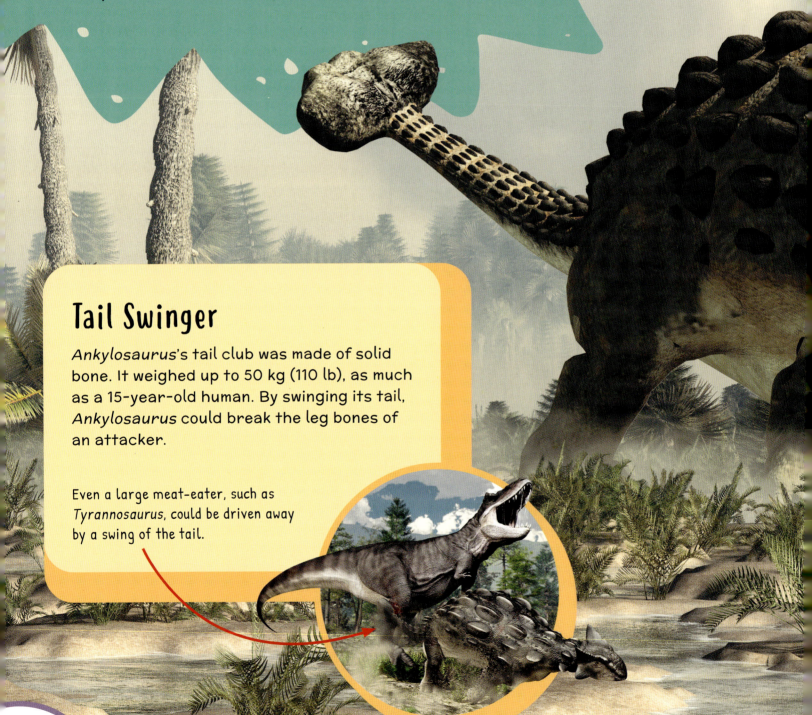

Tail Swinger

Ankylosaurus's tail club was made of solid bone. It weighed up to 50 kg (110 lb), as much as a 15-year-old human. By swinging its tail, *Ankylosaurus* could break the leg bones of an attacker.

Even a large meat-eater, such as *Tyrannosaurus*, could be driven away by a swing of the tail.

The biggest plates were 35 cm (14 in) wide.

Strong Skull

Ankylosaurus means "joined lizard." The bones in this dinosaur's skull were joined together, making it very strong. Extra, flat bones covered the top of its head like tiles.

The skull had an almost triangular shape.

It had four backward-pointing horns.

ANKYLOSAURUS (an-KIH-loh-SORE-us)
HOW BIG: 6 to 8 m (20 to 26 ft) long
HOME: Forests in North America
FOOD: Leaves and fruits
WHEN: 68 to 66 million years ago

FLYING AND SWIMMING REPTILES

The first reptiles lived on land, but over millions of years, some took to the air or water. Their arms evolved into wings or flippers so they could fly or swim. These flyers and swimmers were not dinosaurs, but they could be just as fierce and deadly.

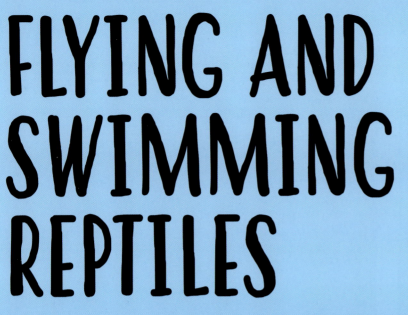

TYLOSAURUS (tile-oh-SORE-us)
HOW BIG: 12 to 14 m (39 to 46 ft) long
HOME: Inland seas in North America
FOOD: Sharks, reptiles, and birds
WHEN: 90 to 66 million years ago

Tylosaurus had gristle between its finger bones, making flippers.

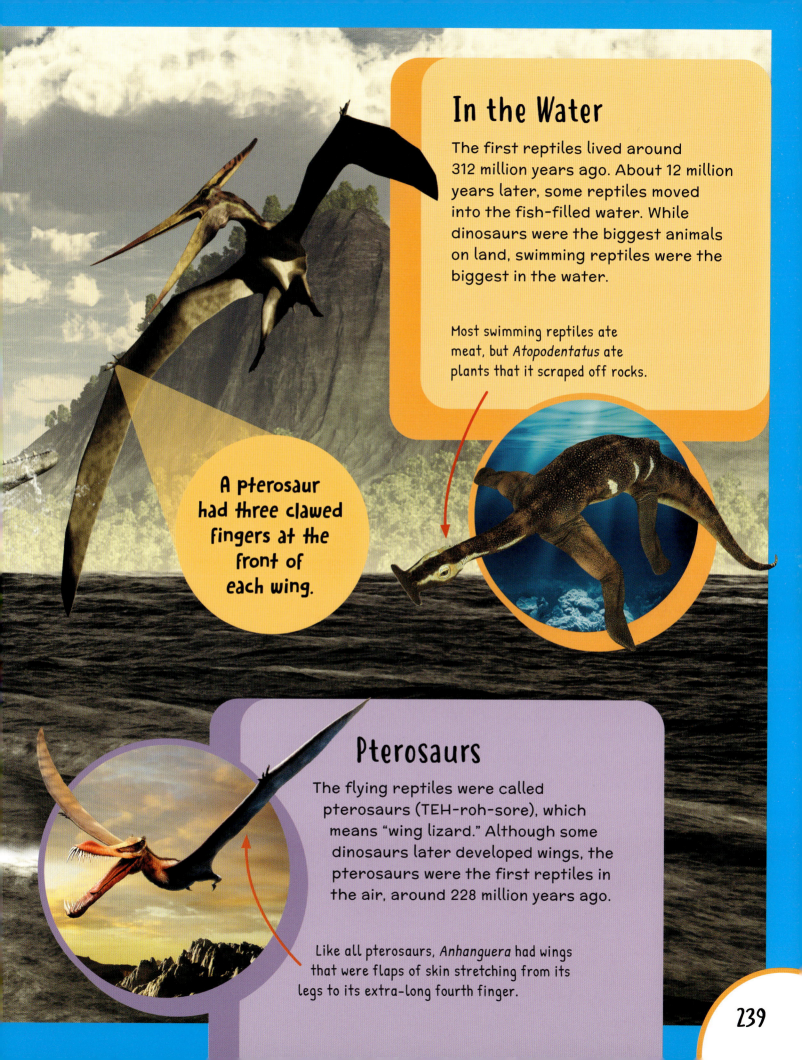

In the Water

The first reptiles lived around 312 million years ago. About 12 million years later, some reptiles moved into the fish-filled water. While dinosaurs were the biggest animals on land, swimming reptiles were the biggest in the water.

Most swimming reptiles ate meat, but *Atopodentatus* ate plants that it scraped off rocks.

A pterosaur had three clawed fingers at the front of each wing.

Pterosaurs

The flying reptiles were called pterosaurs (TEH–roh–sore), which means "wing lizard." Although some dinosaurs later developed wings, the pterosaurs were the first reptiles in the air, around 228 million years ago.

Like all pterosaurs, *Anhanguera* had wings that were flaps of skin stretching from its legs to its extra-long fourth finger.

PTERANODON

Pteranodon's wings were up to 7 m (23 ft) wide, twice as wide as any modern bird's. Broad wings meant *Pteranodon* could glide for long distances without needing to flap. This saved energy as it flew over the ocean in search of fish.

Pteranodon's tall crest was used for attracting a mate.

Fish-Eater

Pteranodon scooped up fish using its long, sharp beak. Food was swallowed whole, as this reptile had no teeth for chewing.

We know *Pteranodon* ate fish, because fossilized fish bones have been found in its fossilized stomach.

Its fourth finger grew up to 1.5 m (5 ft) long.

PTERANODON (teh-RAH-no-don)
HOW BIG: 2 to 3 m (6.5 to 10 ft) long
HOME: Inland seas in North America
FOOD: Fish and other sea creatures
WHEN: 86 to 85 million years ago

All Fours

Like all flying reptiles, *Pteranodon* walked on all fours on land. It took off by jumping into the air, using the strength of its arms and legs together, then flapping upward.

Pteranodon had large hands and feet, which stopped it sinking into wet ground.

QUETZALCOATLUS

Quetzalcoatlus was the largest pterosaur and the largest flying animal ever known to live. It was named after Quetzalcoatl, the feathered serpent god of the Aztecs, a people who lived in Central America in the fourteenth and fifteenth centuries.

Stabbing Beak

Quetzalcoatlus had a very long, sharp beak. Together with the pterosaur's long neck, this would have been useful for stabbing and grabbing small animals that tried to run or hide.

The beak had no teeth, but was edged with hard horn.

Its long neck let *Quetzalcoatlus* probe for prey underwater.

On all fours, it was 3 m (10 ft) high at the shoulder.

End of the Pterosaurs

Along with all other living pterosaurs, *Quetzalcoatlus* died out 66 million years ago when an asteroid hit Earth. Since then, no reptile has flown, unless we count the dinosaurs that had evolved into birds!

The largest *Quetzalcoatlus* had wings 11 m (36 ft) wide, letting it fly far and high.

QUETZALCOATLUS (KWETS-ul-koh-At-lus)
HOW BIG: 5 to 9 m (16 to 30 ft) long
HOME: Plains and swamps in North America
FOOD: Small animals
WHEN: 68 to 66 million years ago

KRONOSAURUS

This huge hunter weighed up to 12 tonnes (13 tons)—as much as six family cars. It was an apex predator, which means that no other predator was large enough to attack it. *Kronosaurus* was named after the powerful Greek god Kronos.

Its massive skull grew up to 285 cm (112 in) long.

Reptile-Eater

Kronosaurus had cone-shaped teeth up to 30 cm (12 in) long. Its crocodile-like jaws could open wide—and snap shut hard. This meant it could crush to death other swimming reptiles.

Kronosaurus ate ichthyosaurs and other swimming reptiles.

Its body was smoothly shaped, to slide easily through water.

Strong Swimmer

The bones and muscles of this reptile's flippers and joints were very strong. *Kronosaurus* was able to push hard against the water with its flippers, reaching a top speed of 10 km/h (6 miles per hour).

It swam faster than the quickest human swimmer.

KRONOSAURUS (CRONE-oh-SORE-us)
HOW BIG: 9 to 11 m (30 to 36 ft) long
HOME: Inland seas in Australia and South America
FOOD: Swimming reptiles
WHEN: 120 to 100 million years ago

MOSASAURUS

Mosasaurus was one of the largest swimming reptiles that ever lived, reaching 17 m (56 ft) long. With its big eyes, it could spot distant prey as it swam in the sunlit surface waters of the ocean. It could kill almost any animal, by cutting and crushing prey with its huge jaws.

Losing Teeth

Mosasaurus teeth were constantly replaced. New teeth were always growing inside the roots of the old teeth. Human children grow their adult teeth in a similar way, with the new teeth pushing out the baby teeth.

These *Mosasaurus* teeth are sharp and cone-shaped, making them perfect for cutting through flesh.

It swam fast by waving its tail from side to side.

Disaster!

When an asteroid hit Earth 66 million years ago, the explosion made ocean water more acidic. This damaged the shells of little ocean animals—and killed them. The animals that fed on shellfish died, followed by the big animals that ate them, like *Mosasaurus*.

Mosasaurus ate smaller reptiles and fish, which in turn fed on shelled animals.

Its jaws opened wide enough to swallow prey whole.

MOSASAURUS (MOH-sah-SORE-us)
HOW BIG: 7 to 17 m (23 to 56 ft) long
HOME: Atlantic Ocean
FOOD: Fish, octopus, birds, and reptiles
WHEN: 82 to 66 million years ago

GLOSSARY

abdomen
The third, back part of an insect's body.

acidic
Able to wear away some materials.

active volcano
A volcano that has had at least one eruption in the last 10,000 years.

algae
Simple plants and plant-like living things that usually live in and around water, such as seaweeds.

amphibian
An animal that is born in water and breathes underwater using gills when young. As an adult, it usually breathes air using lungs, and lives on land or in water.

antenna (antennae)
A slender "feeler" found on the head of some invertebrates.

arachnid
An invertebrate with eight legs and a body in two parts.

asteroid
A small rocky or metal object that orbits the Sun.

astronaut
A person who is trained to travel in a spacecraft.

astronomer
A scientist who studies the stars, planets, and other objects in space.

atmosphere
The gases that surround Earth.

atom
The smallest part of any substance able to exist on its own.

axis
An imaginary straight line through a planet or moon, around which the object turns.

bacteria
Simple living things that are so small they can be seen only under a microscope.

bask
To rest in the sunshine.

black hole
An area of space with such strong gravity that no object—or light—can escape its pull.

caecilian
A worm-like amphibian that spends most of its life underground.

camouflage
The way the shade and shape of an animal make it less visible in its habitat.

cartilage
A strong but bendy material found in the body of some animals.

climate
The usual weather in an area, year after year.

comet
A small icy object with an elliptical (stretched-out) orbit that takes it both close to and far from the Sun.

condense
To turn from a gas into a liquid.

coniferous forest
An area with many trees that have needle-shaped leaves, which do not fall from the tree before winter.

constellation
A group of stars that seem to make a pattern in the night sky, when viewed from Earth.

constriction
Squeezing and tightening.

continent
A large area of land, usually separated from other continents by ocean.

coral reef
An area, usually in warm, shallow seawater, where thousands of tiny coral animals live. Their bony skeletons make a rock-like ridge on the seafloor.

core
The innermost part of a planet, star, or moon.

crater
A round dip in the ground, made when a volcano erupts then partly collapses, or in the surface of a planet or moon, made by a space rock hitting it.

crest
A growth of bone, scales, feathers, skin, or hair on the heads or backs of some animals.

crust
The outer layer of a planet or moon.

day
The time taken for a planet to turn around its axis, so the Sun appears to return to the same position in the sky. Daytime is the portion of a day when part of the planet is facing the Sun.

desert
An area where there is very little rain, so not many plants can grow.

dinosaur
A group of reptiles that lived between 243 and 66 million years ago. Today's reptiles include lizards and snakes.

dwarf planet
A rounded object that orbits a star, but is not large enough for its gravity to clear other objects out of its orbit.

earthquake
A shaking of the ground caused by the movement of Earth's tectonic plates.

eclipse
When a star, planet, or moon is hidden by another large object moving between it and the watcher, or when a star, planet or moon moves into the shadow of another object.

equator
An invisible line around the middle of a planet, dividing it into northern and southern halves.

eruption
When lava, gas, or ash spill out of a volcano.

evaporate
To turn from a liquid into a gas.

evolve
To change over millions of years. An animal's body and habits may change slowly to suit the weather and landscape, or to better attack or escape from other animals.

exoplanet
A planet outside our Solar System.

exoskeleton
The hard outer covering of some invertebrates. As the animal grows, it must shed its old exoskeleton and grow a new one.

extinction
When the last living member of an animal or plant species dies.

family
A group of species that are closely related to each other, so they look and behave quite similarly.

fang
A large, sharp tooth.

feather
A light, fringed growth from the skin of birds and some dinosaurs. A feather has a tough central stem, with softer threads growing from either side. Feathers are made from keratin, also called horn—the same material that is found in scales and human hair.

fin
A body part that sticks out from the body of fish and some other water-living animals, helping them swim.

flipper
A wide, flat, leg-like body part, used for swimming.

forest
A large area of land with many trees that are growing closely together.

fossil
The remains of an animal or plant that died thousands or millions of years ago.

freshwater
Unsalted water, such as rivers, lakes, and ponds.

fuel
A material that can be burned to make heat.

galaxy
Thousands, millions, or billions of stars, as well as gas and dust, that are held together by gravity.

gas
A substance, such as air, that can move around freely and has no fixed shape.

gill
A body part in fish and amphibians that takes oxygen from water.

glide
To move smoothly through the air, without flapping wings.

grassland
A large area of land covered by grasses.

gravity
A force that pulls all objects toward each other. The larger the object, the stronger the pull of its gravity.

habitat
The natural home of an animal, plant, or other living thing.

helium
The second most common type of atom in the Universe. Helium is a gas at a normal room temperature.

hemisphere
Half of a ball-shaped object, such as a planet or moon.

horn
A tough, hard material, also called keratin, that is found in scales, feathers, beaks, claws, nails, and hair. Another meaning of "horn" is a pointed, bony growth on the head.

hover
Stay in one place in the air.

hydrogen
The most common type of atom in the Universe. Hydrogen is a gas at a normal room temperature.

infrared
A type of energy that is invisible to human eyes but can be felt as warmth.

inject
To press inside the body.

insect
An invertebrate with six legs and a body in three parts: head, thorax, and abdomen.

invertebrate
An animal without a backbone, such as a crab, spider, or insect.

larva (larvae)
A young stage in the life cycle of some invertebrates and amphibians. As a larva, the animal looks very different from how it looks as an adult.

lava
Melted rock that spills out of a volcano above ground.

light year
The distance that light travels in a year: 9.46 trillion km (5.88 trillion miles).

limb
An arm, leg, or wing.

liquid
A substance that flows and can be poured.

lungs
Body parts that take oxygen from air. Lungs are found in mammals, reptiles, birds, and most adult amphibians.

lure
A body part that attracts other animals.

magma
Melted rock inside Earth.

mammal
An animal that grows hair at some point in its life and feeds its babies on milk.

mandible
A jaw, normally used for biting.

mantle
The layer inside a planet or moon that lies between the crust and the core.

mass
A measure of the amount of material in an object.

metallic
Behaving like a metal by letting electricity flow through it.

metamorphosis
The change in body shape and lifestyle that some animals go through as they grow into adults. Amphibians and some invertebrates go through metamorphosis.

meteor
A portion of a comet, asteroid, or other space object that is glowing as it travels through Earth's atmosphere; also known as a shooting star.

migrate
To move from one area to another, usually at the same time every year.

mineral
A solid made when elements join together in a regular pattern.

moon
A large, rocky or icy object that orbits a planet; Earth has one moon.

mucus
A slimy substance made by some animals.

nectar
A sugary liquid made by flowers.

nocturnal
Awake and active during the night.

nodosaur
A plant-eating dinosaur with a heavy body covered in bony plates.

nutrient
A material that helps a living thing grow and live.

orbit
The curved path of an object around a star, planet, or moon.

oxygen
The third most common type of atom in the Universe. Oxygen is a gas at a normal room temperature and is also part of water. Animals need oxygen to live.

particle
A tiny portion of a substance.

pedipalps
A pair of leg-like body parts found on spiders and scorpions. In spiders, they are feelers, but in scorpions they are pincers.

pigmentation
The natural shade of animal or plant tissue.

plain
A large area of flat land.

planet
A large, rounded object that orbits the Sun or another star. Its gravity is strong enough to clear objects out of its orbit.

plate
A bony, shield-like structure that grows from deep within an animal's skin. The skin that grows over a plate is often covered by horn.

pole
A point at the most northerly or most southerly end of a planet, moon, or star.

pollen
A powder made by flowers. It can fertilize other flowers of the same species so that they make seeds.

polyp
The life stage of some invertebrates, such as jellyfish, during which the animal does not move.

precipitation
Water that falls from clouds toward the ground, often as rain or snow.

predator
An animal that hunts other animals.

prey
An animal that is killed by another animal for food.

primate
A group of mammals that includes monkeys, apes, and humans.

pterosaur
An extinct reptile with wings attached to its extra-long fourth fingers. A pterosaur was a relative of dinosaurs.

rain forest
A thick forest found in tropical areas where it is hot and rainy.

relative
An animal that is a member of the same family or group of similar animals.

reptile
An animal with dry, scaly skin that usually lays eggs on land.

rock
A solid that is a mixture of minerals.

rocket
A vehicle with a powerful engine that burns fuel to make a blast of hot gas, which sends the rocket in the opposite direction (up).

rotation
Turning around an axis.

rover
A robot that can travel across the surface of a planet, moon, or other space object.

satellite
A human-made object that is placed in orbit around a planet or moon. Any object that orbits a larger object may also be known as a satellite.

sauropod
A plant-eating dinosaur with a long neck and a long tail.

scale
A small bony plate that protects the skin of most fish and reptiles.

seawater
Salty water in the sea or ocean.

seismologist
A scientist who studies earthquakes.

shield volcano
A wide volcano with gently sloping sides.

shoal
A large number of fish that are swimming together.

shock wave
A wave of shaking that travels out from an earthquake or explosion.

shrub
A plant, smaller than a tree, that has lots of woody stems.

snout
Found in animals such as dogs and crocodiles, it is the area of the face that sticks out, made up of the nose and mouth.

solar panel
A device that turns sunlight into electricity.

Solar System
The eight planets and the smaller rocky or icy objects that travel around the Sun.

space capsule
A wingless spacecraft, often used to carry a human crew.

spacecraft
A vehicle used for journeying in space.

space probe
A spacecraft that travels through space collecting scientific information to send back to Earth. It has no human crew.

space station
A large satellite that can be lived and worked in for long periods of time.

species
A group of living things that look similar and can make babies together.

spine
A long, pointed bone or body part. Another meaning of "spine" is an animal's backbone.

spring
A place where water flows out of the ground.

star
A huge ball of burning gas in space.

stratovolcano
A tall, steep-sided volcano.

Sun
The star at the middle of our Solar System, around which Earth and the other planets orbit.

swamp
An area of low land where water collects, making it wet and soft.

telescope
An instrument designed to make distant objects appear nearer, using mirrors and lenses to collect and focus light.

temperate
In the areas midway between the poles and the equator, where it does not get very hot or very cold.

tentacle
A long, thin body part, used for feeling or grabbing.

theropod
A meat-eating dinosaur that usually walked on its two back legs, had hollow bones and, usually, three main toes.

thorax
The middle part of an insect's body. The legs are attached to the thorax.

tropical
The area around the equator, where it is warm all year.

tsunami
A tall ocean wave caused by an underwater earthquake, eruption, or rock slide.

tundra
A region where it is too cold for trees to grow and the ground is always partly frozen.

Universe
All of space and its contents, including planets, stars, galaxies, and all other objects and energy.

venomous
Able to give a poisoned bite or sting.

vent
An opening in a volcano through which lava, gas, or ash can spill out.

visible Universe
The part of the Universe that we can see from Earth.

volcano
A hole in a planet or moon's surface through which melted rock named lava can spill out.

water vapor
Water in the form of an invisible gas.

weather
What is happening in the air above Earth, such as wind, rain, and temperature.

wetland
Land, such as swamps and marshes, that is soggy or covered by water.

wild
Living free, not kept by humans.

wildfire
A fire that spreads through forests, woods, or grassland.

woodland
Land with many trees and other plants. The trees are far enough apart for sunlight to reach the ground in places.

year
The time taken for Earth to complete one orbit around the Sun.

INDEX

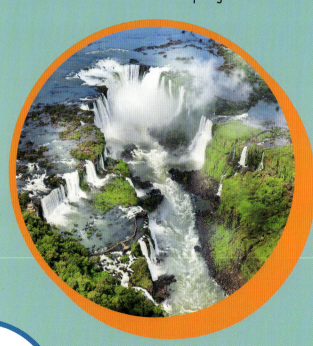

PICTURE CREDITS

Every attempt has been made to clear copyright. If there are any inadvertent omissions, please apply to the publisher for rectification.
Key: b = bottom, t = top, c = center, l = left, r = right